Assessment Guide

Grade 4

HOUGHTON MIFFLIN HARCOURT

Acknowledgments for Cover Photos

Front Cover: *stingray* ©Jeffrey L. Rotman/Corbis; *moth* ©Millard H. Sharp/Photo Researchers, Inc.; *astronaut* ©NASA; *thermometer* ©StockImages/Alamy; *robotic arm* ©Garry Gay/The Image Bank/ Getty Images.

Contents

Overview

ScienceFusion provides parallel instructional paths for meeting the Next Generation Sunshine State Science Standards and Benchmarks. You may choose to use the print path, digital path, or a combination of both. The quizzes, tests, and other resources in this Assessment Guide may be used with any path you choose.

The *ScienceFusion* assessment options are intended to give you maximum flexibility in assessing what your students know and can do. The program's formative, summative, and performance assessment categories reflect the understanding that assessment is a learning opportunity for students and that all students must demonstrate standards mastery at the end of a school year. Florida has reduced the number of science benchmarks in the Next Generation Sunshine State Standards, allowing you to spend more time on the shorter list of topics. With fewer benchmarks to cover than in previous years, the assessments are also very focused and concise.

Formative Assessment

At the end of each lesson in the Student Edition, the Brain Check will help you evaluate how well students grasped the concepts taught. The opportunities for students to annotate their Student Edition, including the Active Reading features, can also provide insight into how well students are learning the concepts.

Opportunities are provided throughout the program for students to check their progress and understanding. At the end of each digital unit, a student self-assessment prompts students to return to areas in which they may need additional work.

The Teacher Edition offers a number of additional tools for formative assessment. Look for the science note-booking strategies Generate Ideas and Summarize Ideas that begin and end many of the two-page sections of the lessons. These strategies provide numerous ways to informally assess whether students are remembering what they read and getting the main ideas. Questions that address a variety of dimensions—including concept development, inquiry skills, and use of reading strategies—are strategically placed throughout each lesson. Located in this Assessment Guide is yet another tool, the Observation Checklist, on which you can record observations of students' ability to use science inquiry skills.

Summative Assessment

To help you reinforce and assess mastery of unit objectives, *ScienceFusion* includes both reviews and tests. You will find the Unit Benchmark Reviews in the Student Edition. Lesson Quizzes and Unit Benchmark Tests are provided in this Assessment Guide. All of these assessment tools are in multiple-choice formats that mirror Florida statewide assessment formats. Also included in this Assessment Guide are Benchmark Practice Tests that provide items for all the science benchmarks in the Next Generation Sunshine State Standards.

Performance Assessment

Performance tasks provide evidence of students' ability to use science inquiry skills and critical thinking to complete an authentic task. A brief performance task is included in the Teacher Edition with each Unit Benchmark Review. A more comprehensive performance task is provided for each unit in this Assessment Guide. Each includes teacher directions and a scoring rubric.

Self-Assessment and Portfolio Assessment

Students should be challenged to reflect on their work and monitor their learning. Several checklists are provided for this purpose. Self-Assessment—Active Reading, Experiment/Project Summary Sheet, Self-Assessment—Science Notebook, Science Experiences Record, and Guide to My Science Portfolio can be used by students to describe or evaluate their own experiences and projects. Opportunities for self-assessment and evaluation are embedded at key points on the digital path.

Online Assessment

All of the quizzes and tests within this Assessment Guide are available in computer-scored format with the *ScienceFusion* online resources. Banks of items from which tests can be built are also available.

Test-Taking Tips

Understandably, students often experience test-related anxiety. Teaching students to apply a number of general test-taking strategies may bolster their confidence and result in improved student performance on formal assessment. As students take a test, they should

- scan the entire test first before answering any questions.

- read the directions slowly and carefully before beginning a section.

- begin with the easiest questions or most familiar material.

- read the question and all answer options before selecting an answer.

- watch out for key words such as *not, least, best, most,* and so on.

- carefully analyze graphs, tables, diagrams, and pictures that accompany items.

- double-check answers to catch and correct errors.

- erase all mistakes completely and write corrections neatly.

Test Preparation

Students perform better on formal assessments when they are well prepared for the testing situation. Here are some things you can do before a test to help your students do their best work.

- Explain the nature of the test to students.

- Suggest that they review the questions at the end of the lessons and the chapter.

- Remind students to get a good night's sleep before the test.

- Discuss why they should eat a balanced meal beforehand.

- Encourage students to relax while they take the test.

Performance Assessment

Teachers today have come to realize that the multiple-choice format of traditional tests, while useful and efficient, cannot provide a complete picture of students' growth in science. Standardized multiple-choice tests cannot fully reveal how students *think and do things*—an essential aspect of science literacy. Performance assessment can provide this missing information and help balance your assessment program. Well-constructed performance assessments provide a window through which teachers may view students' thought processes.

An important feature of performance assessment is that it involves a hands-on activity in which students solve a situational problem. Students often find performance assessment more enjoyable than traditional paper-and-pencil tests. Another advantage is that it models good instruction: students are assessed as they learn and learn as they are assessed.

Performance Assessment in *ScienceFusion*

Performance tasks can be found in two locations in *ScienceFusion*. In the **Teacher Edition,** a brief performance task is part of the information that accompanies each Benchmark Review. In this **Assessment Guide,** a more comprehensive task follows each Unit Benchmark Test. Both types of performance tasks will provide insights into students' ability to apply key science inquiry skills and concepts taught in the unit.

Administering Performance Tasks

Unlike traditional assessment tools, performance assessment does not provide standardized directions for its administration or impose specific time limits on students, although a suggested time frame is offered as a guideline. The suggestions that follow may help you define your role in this assessment.

- *Be prepared.*
  A few days before students begin the task, read the Teacher's Directions and gather the materials needed.

- *Be clear.*
  Explain the directions for the task; rephrase them as needed. Also, explain how students' performance will be evaluated. Show students the rubric you plan to use, and explain the performance indicators in language your students understand.

- *Be encouraging.*
  Your role in administering the assessments should be that of a coach—motivating, guiding, and encouraging students to produce their best work.

- *Be supportive.*
  You may assist students who need help. The amount of assistance needed will depend on the needs and abilities of individual students.

- *Be flexible.*
  Not all students need to proceed through the performance task at the same rate and in the same manner. Allow students adequate time to do their best work.

- *Involve students in evaluation.*
  Invite students to join you as partners in the evaluation process, particularly in development or modification of the rubric.

Rubrics for Assessing Performance

A well-written rubric can help you score students' work accurately and fairly. Moreover, a rubric gives students a better idea of what qualities their work should exhibit before they begin a task.

Each performance task in the program has its own rubric. The rubric lists performance indicators, which are brief statements of what to look for in assessing the skills and understandings that the task addresses. A sample rubric for a task in this **Assessment Guide** follows.

Scoring Rubric

Performance Indicators

_____ Assembles the kite successfully.

_____ Carries out the experiment daily.

_____ Records results accurately.

_____ Makes an accurate chart and uses it to report the strength of wind observed each day.

Observations and Rubric Score

3	2	1	0

Scoring a Performance Task

The scoring system used for performance tasks in this **Assessment Guide** is a 4-point scale that is compatible with those used by many state assessment programs. You may wish to modify the rubrics as a 3- or 5-point scale. To determine a student's score on a performance task, review the indicators checked on the rubric and then select the score that best represents the student's overall performance on the task.

4-Point Scale			
Excellent Achievement	Adequate Achievement	Limited Achievement	Little or No Achievement
3	2	1	0

How to Convert a Rubric Score into a Grade

If, for grading purposes, you want to record a letter or numerical grade rather than a holistic score for the student's performance on a task, you can use the following conversion table.

Holistic Score	Letter Grade	Numerical Grade
3	A	90–100
2	B	80–89
1	C	70–79
0	D–F	69 or below

Developing Your Own Rubric

From time to time, you may want to either develop your own rubric or work together with your students to create one. Research has shown that significantly improved performance can result from student participation in the construction of rubrics.

Developing a rubric for a performance task involves three basic steps: (1) Identify the inquiry skills that are taught in the chapter and that students must perform to complete the task successfully, and identify what understanding of content is also required. (2) Determine which skills and understandings are involved in each step. (3) Decide what you will look for to confirm that the student has acquired each skill and understanding you identified.

Classroom Observation

"Kid watching" is a natural part of teaching and an important part of evaluation. The purpose of classroom observation in assessment is to gather and record information that can lead to improved instruction. In this booklet, you will find an Observation Checklist (p. AG xiii) on which you can record noteworthy observations of students' ability to use science inquiry skills.

Using the Observation Checklist

- *Identify the skills you will observe.*
  Find out which inquiry skills are introduced and reinforced in the chapter.

- *Focus on only a few students at a time.*
  You will find this more effective than trying to observe the entire class at once.

- *Look for a pattern.*
  It is important to observe a student's strengths and weaknesses over a period of time to determine whether a pattern exists.

- *Plan how and when to record observations.*
  Decide whether to

  —record observations immediately on the checklist as you move about the room or

  —make jottings or mental notes of observations and record them later.

- *Don't agonize over the ratings.*
  Students who stand out as particularly strong will clearly merit a rating of 3 ("Outstanding"). Others may clearly earn a rating of 1 ("Needs Improvement"). This doesn't mean, however, that a 2 ("Satisfactory") is automatically the appropriate rating for the rest of the class. For example, you may not have had sufficient opportunity to observe a student demonstrate certain skills. The checklist cells for these skills should remain blank under the student's name until you have observed him or her perform the skills.

- *Review your checklist periodically, and ask yourself questions such as these:*

  What are the student's strongest/weakest attributes?

  In what ways has the student shown growth?

  In what areas does the class as a whole show strength/weakness?

  What kinds of activities would encourage growth?

  Do I need to allot more time to classroom observation?

- *Use the data you collect.*

  Refer to your classroom observation checklists when you plan lessons, form groups, assign grades, and confer with students and family members.

Date _____

	Rating Scale		
3	Outstanding	1	Needs Improvement
2	Satisfactory		Not Enough Opportunity to Observe

Names of Students

Inquiry Skills										
Observe										
Compare										
Classify/Order										
Gather, Record, Display, or Interpret Data										
Use Numbers										
Communicate										
Plan and Conduct Simple Investigations										
Measure										
Predict										
Infer										
Draw Conclusions										
Use Time/Space Relationships										
Hypothesize										
Formulate or Use Models										
Identify and Control Variables										
Experiment										

Using Student Self-Assessment

Researchers have evidence that self-evaluation and the reflection it involves can have positive effects on students' learning. To achieve these effects, students must be challenged to reflect on their work and to monitor, analyze, and control their own learning—beginning in the earliest grades.

Frequent opportunities for students to evaluate their performance build the skills and confidence they need for effective self-assessment. A trusting relationship between the student and the teacher is also essential. Students must be assured that honest responses can have only a positive effect on the teacher's view of them and that responses will not be used to determine grades.

Two checklists are found in this **Assessment Guide.** One is Self-Assessment—Active Reading: a form that leads students to reflect on and evaluate their role as active readers. The second is the Experiment/Project Summary Sheet—a form to help students describe and evaluate any projects or activities they may have designed or conducted as independent inquiry.

Using Self-Assessment Forms

- *Explain the directions.*
  Discuss the forms and how to complete them.

- *Encourage honest responses.*
  Be sure to tell students that there are no "right" responses to the items.

- *Model the process.*
  One way to foster candid responses is to model the process yourself, including at least one response that is not positive. Discuss reasons for your responses.

- *Be open to variations in students' responses.*
  Negative responses should not be viewed as indicating weaknesses. Rather, they confirm that you did a good job of communicating the importance of honesty in self-assessment.

- *Discuss responses with students.*
  You may wish to clarify students' responses in conferences with them and in family conferences. Invite both students and family members to help you plan activities for school and home that will motivate and support students' growth in science.

Name _____

Think About It

To find out if you are an Active Reader, write "yes" if a sentence describes what you did when you read the lesson.

_____ 1. Every page or two I stopped to think about what I had read to be sure I understood it.

_____ 2. I followed the Active Reading directions in each lesson.

_____ 3. When I did not understand something, I put a question mark in the margin so I would remember to ask about it.

_____ 4. I paused to study the photographs, diagrams, and charts on every page.

_____ 5. I recorded notes on the pages of my book to help me remember key ideas.

_____ 6. I used the Answer Key in Sum It Up and made sure all my answers were correct.

_____ 7. I used my notes and Active Reading marks as a study guide for tests.

This is how being an Active Reader helped me.

_____

_____

_____

_____

_____

This is what I will do to be a more Active Reader next time.

_____

_____

_____

_____

Name _____

My Experiment/Project

You can tell about your science project or experiment by completing the following sentences.

1. My experiment/project was about _____

    _____

    _____

2. I worked on this experiment/project with _____

    _____

    _____

3. I gathered information from these sources: _____

    _____

    _____

4. The most important thing I learned from doing this experiment/project is _____

    _____

    _____

5. I think I did a (an) _____ job on my experiment/project because _____

    _____

    _____

6. I'd also like to tell you _____

    _____

    _____

    _____

    _____

    _____

Name _____

Think About It

Do you keep a Science Notebook? Write "yes" if a sentence describes your Science Notebook.

_____ 1. I am building a table of contents in the first four pages of my notebook. I add entries throughout the year.

_____ 2. I am building an index in the back of my notebook. I add entries throughout the year.

_____ 3. I write my plans for investigations in my notebook. My plans include questions I want to investigate and the procedure I will follow.

_____ 4. I record results, notes, and data from my investigations.

_____ 5. I use my notebook to record science notes, drawings, and graphic organizers.

_____ 6. I include the date and a title with each entry in my notebook.

_____ 7. I use my notebook to review and reflect on what I have learned.

This is how keeping a Science Notebook is helping me.

_____

_____

_____

_____

_____

_____

_____

This is what I will do to improve my Science Notebook.

_____

_____

_____

_____

_____

_____

_____

Portfolio Assessment

A portfolio is a showcase for student work, a place where many types of assignments, projects, reports, and writings can be collected. The work samples in the collection provide "snapshots" of the student's efforts over time, and taken together they reveal the student's growth, attitudes, and understanding better than any other type of assessment. However, portfolios are not ends in themselves. Their value comes from creating them, discussing them, and using them to improve learning.

The purpose of using portfolios in science is threefold:

- *To give the student a voice in the assessment process.*

- *To foster reflection, self-monitoring, and self-evaluation.*

- *To provide a comprehensive picture of a student's progress.*

Portfolio Assessment in *ScienceFusion*

In *ScienceFusion*, students may assemble portfolio collections of their work. The collection may include a few required papers, such as tests, performance tasks, lab response pages, and Experiment/Project Evaluation forms.

From time to time, consider including other measures (Science Experiences Record, Self-Assessment—Active Reading, Self-Assessment—Science Notebook). The Science Experiences Record, for example, can reveal insights about student interests, ideas, and out-of-school experiences (museum visits, nature walks, outside readings, and so on) that otherwise you might not know about. Materials to help you and your students build portfolios and use them for evaluation are included in the pages that follow.

Using Portfolio Assessment

- *Explain the portfolio and its use.*
  Describe how people in many fields use portfolios to present samples of their work when they are applying for a job. Tell students that they can create their own portfolio to show what they have learned, what skills they have acquired, and how they think they are doing in science.

- *Decide what standard pieces should be included.*
  Encourage students to identify a few standard, or "required," work samples that they will include in their portfolios, and discuss reasons for including them. The Student Task sheets for the performance assessments in this **Assessment Guide,** for example, might be a standard sample in the portfolios because they show students' ability to use inquiry skills and critical thinking skills. Together with your class, decide on the required work samples that everyone's portfolio will include.

- *Discuss student-selected work samples.*
  Point out that the best work to select is not necessarily the longest or the neatest. Rather, it is work the student believes will best demonstrate his or her growth in science understanding and skills.

- *Establish a basic plan.*
  Decide about how many work samples will be included in the portfolio and when they should be selected. Ask students to list on the Guide to My Science Portfolio (p. AG xxi) each sample they select and to explain why they selected it.

- *Tell students how you will evaluate their portfolios.*
  Use a blank Portfolio Evaluation sheet to explain how you will evaluate the contents of a portfolio.

- *Use the portfolio.*
  Use the portfolio as a handy reference tool in determining students' science grades and in holding conferences with them and family members. You may wish to send the portfolio home for family members to review.

Name _____

My Science Experiences

Date	What I Did	What I Thought or Learned

Name _____

My Science Portfolio

What Is in My Portfolio	Why I Chose It
1.	
2.	
3.	
4.	
5.	
6.	
7.	

I organized my Science Portfolio this way because _____

_____

_____

_____

_____

AG xxi

Grade 4 • Assessment Guide • Florida

Name _____ Date _____

Portfolio Evaluation

Aspects of Science Literacy	Evidence of Growth
1. Understands science concepts *(Animals, Plants; Earth's Land, Air, Water; Space; Weather; Matter, Motion, Energy)*	_____ _____ _____
2. Uses inquiry skills *(observes, compares, classifies, gathers/ interprets data, communicates, measures, experiments, infers, predicts, draws conclusions)*	_____ _____ _____
3. Thinks critically *(analyzes, synthesizes, evaluates, applies ideas effectively, solves problems)*	_____ _____ _____
4. Displays traits/attitudes of a scientist *(is curious, questioning, persistent, precise, creative, enthusiastic; uses science materials carefully; is concerned for environment)*	_____ _____ _____

Summary of Portfolio Assessment

For This Review			Since Last Review		
Excellent	Good	Fair	Improving	About the Same	Not as Good

What Do Scientists Do?

1 Scientists make observations, conduct experiments, and draw conclusions. Which statement is true of **all** scientists?

(A) Scientists study living things.

(B) Scientists study the natural world.

(C) Scientists study items found on Earth.

(D) Scientists study things found in outer space.

2 Kim places a cup of water and a cup of cooking oil in the freezer. Every 30 min, Kim checks the cups. She records the time when the liquid in each cup freezes. Which question is Kim investigating?

(F) Which liquid freezes faster, water or cooking oil?

(G) Which liquid tastes better frozen, water or cooking oil?

(H) Which item floats better, frozen water or frozen cooking oil?

(I) Which item melts faster, frozen water or frozen cooking oil?

3 Kwan asks people in his class to report how many times per week they recycle. Kwan asks friends in two other classes to collect reports from their classmates, too. What is **true** about Kwan's investigation?

(A) It involves collaboration.

(B) It follows the scientific method.

(C) It produces results that don't change.

(D) It explains why people recycle.

4 Franz wants to investigate moon craters. He drips water into a shallow pan of flour. He holds the dropper at a different height each time he moves to a new area of the pan. Franz observes that the water drops make dents of differing sizes in the flour. Which type of experiment is Franz conducting?

(F) modeling   (H) classifying

(G) surveying   (I) directly studying

5 A scientist looks at a graph of the results of his experiment. He draws a conclusion about the results. What is one way the scientist uses his conclusion?

(A) to decide whether his results are correct

(B) to decide whether his hypothesis is correct

(C) to decide whether he should make a different conclusion

(D) to decide whether he should share his results with others

What Skills Do Scientists Use?

1 During Carmela's investigation, a plant grew 1 in. each week for 4 weeks. When she displays her drawing of the weekly changes in the size of the plant, what skill is she using?

- (A) communication
- (B) inference
- (C) observation
- (D) variables

2 Sarah is studying water. She thinks that adding salt to water may make it freeze at a higher temperature. Which word describes her statement?

- (F) conclusion
- (G) hypothesis
- (H) investigation
- (I) variable

3 Emily grew one plant on the window sill. She grew another plant inside a black plastic bag. She made a poster about how the plants grew. What does Emily's poster do?

- (A) predicts the data
- (B) classifies the data
- (C) hypothesizes the data
- (D) communicates the data

4 Nicholas wants to add more blueberries to a muffin recipe. He thinks it will make the muffins taste better. What part of the inquiry process are the blueberries?

- (F) variable
- (G) question
- (H) hypothesis
- (I) conclusion

5 Connor and Dylan studied how far two toy pull-back cars travel. Each student pulled a car back and let it go. Then they measured how far each car traveled before it stopped. What part of the inquiry process did the students do?

- (A) made a prediction
- (B) drew a conclusion
- (C) conducted an investigation
- (D) communicated their results

How Do Scientists Collect and Use Data?

❶ Kiera is planning an investigation of fossils that scientists have found where she lives in Florida. Which would be her **best** source of information?

(A) science dictionary

(B) book about dinosaurs

(C) local science museum

(D) television show about rocks

❷ Michi places a beaker of water in sunlight and measures how the water temperature changes. Which unit of measurement will Michi use to record his data?

(F) grams

(G) centimeters

(H) degrees Celsius

(I) cubic centimeters

❸ Students in Zoe's class measure the time it takes a toy car to move along a track. Why should Zoe compare her data to other students' data?

(A) to choose the best time to record

(B) to see if she needs to change her data

(C) to decide why the car moved slowly

(D) to see if her data match other students' data

❹ Lataya collects one leaf from each tree around the school. What would be the **best** way for Lataya to find out which leaf has the greatest mass?

(F) Hold the leaves, two at a time, in her hands.

(G) Find the mass of each leaf in a pan balance.

(H) Lay each leaf on a table beside a measuring tape.

(I) Hang all of the leaves together from a spring scale.

❺ Shawna is studying two types of fish for a project. She draws pictures of the fish.

Clown fish   Boxfish

Which is an observation Shawna might make of the fish?

(A) The boxfish has a funny shape.

(B) Most people have seen pictures of the clown fish.

(C) People will laugh when they see the boxfish picture.

(D) The clown fish has stripes around its head, body, and tail.

Why Do Scientists Compare Results?

❶ Devon, Margarita, Renee, and Malik make muffins. They wonder whose muffins have the greatest diameter. Devon measures the diameter of his muffins with a meter stick. Margarita places jellybeans end to end. Renee uses coins, and Malik uses paper clips. Which method uses a standard measure?

Ⓐ meter stick   Ⓒ jellybeans

Ⓑ coins   Ⓓ paper clips

❷ Ms. Nguyen's science class is studying measurement. She asks the students to measure the distance around a football from tip to tip. Which tool should the students use?

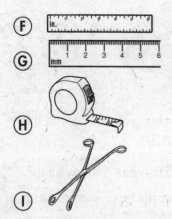

Ⓕ
Ⓖ
Ⓗ
Ⓘ

❸ Four classmates measure the weight of the same sample of rock salt. Which measurement is **most** exact?

Ⓐ 1 kg   Ⓒ 0.894 kg

Ⓑ 0.89 kg   Ⓓ 0.8937 kg

❹ Ms. Ybarra's class is studying how corn plants grow. She asks the students to find ways to measure a plant. Which method of measurement is based on a nonstandard tool?

Ⓕ ruler to measure the length of the roots and stem

Ⓖ scale to weigh the amount of corn that the plant produces

Ⓗ crayons to record how green the plant's leaves are

Ⓘ measuring cup to determine how much water the plant uses

❺ Myrna is making a large batch of chili. The recipe calls for 2 kg of ground beef. She does not have a kitchen scale, and she has a large, unmarked package of beef. Which nonstandard method of measurement will help Myrna determine how much beef is equal to 2 kg?

Ⓐ Fill a 4-qt saucepan with beef.

Ⓑ Compare the weight of the beef to three large apples.

Ⓒ Compare the weight of the beef to a 2-kg package of flour.

Ⓓ Use the same length, width, and height of beef as a large loaf of bread.

What Kinds of Models Do Scientists Use?

1 Thad looks at a photograph of a tadpole. He wonders how the tadpole's body changes as the tadpole grows. What type of model would be **most useful** for Thad to observe?

(A) a set of plastic models of two different types of frogs

(B) a computer animation that follows a frog through its life cycle

(C) a set of diagrams that shows the different parts of a frog's body

(D) a photograph of a tadpole and a photograph of a fully grown frog

2 A scientist plans to create a model of a coral reef. What must the scientist do when building the model?

(F) include the most important parts

(G) use a computer to build the model

(H) build the model the same size as a reef

(I) build the model so that it can be taken apart

3 Scientists use different models depending on the subject they are studying. What is **true** about all models?

(A) Models are made by humans.

(B) Models represent one object at a time.

(C) Models are the same size as the objects they represent.

(D) Models include every detail of the objects they represent.

4 Kate thinks about how to plant a garden. She imagines where the garden will be. She pictures what will grow in her garden and where. Next, Kate draws a picture of her garden. What is Kate doing?

(F) She is creating two kinds of mental models.

(G) She is creating a two-dimensional model from a mental model.

(H) She is creating a three-dimensional model from a mental model.

(I) She is creating a three-dimensional model from a two-dimensional model.

5 Vanessa reads that a bird's bones are hollow, but strong. Vanessa wants to build a three-dimensional model of a bird. Which material would be her **best** choice to use for bones in her model?

(A) toothpicks

(B) modeling clay

(C) blades of grass

(D) drinking straws

How Can You Model the School?

1 Cyrus wants to measure the classroom to create a model of it. Which of the following methods will give the **most** accurate measurement?

Ⓐ use a metric tape measure

Ⓑ measure the room in foot paces

Ⓒ use the same measurements that the class next door used

Ⓓ measure the room using the number of tiles on the floor

2 Four students in Mrs. Mott's class each write an explanation of a 3-D model of a classroom. Their goal is to help people understand how much total space there is in the classroom. Which of the following descriptions accomplishes the goal?

Ⓕ The classroom measures 5 m by 5 m.

Ⓖ The six classroom windows measure 1 m by 1.5 m.

Ⓗ The length of the classroom is 5 m long and 9 m high.

Ⓘ The floor plan measures 5 m by 5 m, and the height is 9 m.

3 Claude made a 2-D model of the length and width of a classroom. Shayne made a 3-D diorama. Which of the following describes how the models are **different**?

Ⓐ Claude's model does not show the sides of the walls of the classroom.

Ⓑ Only Claude could use a meter stick to take measurements for his model.

Ⓒ Only Shayne's model shows the floor of the classroom.

Ⓓ Only Shayne's model shows the length and width of the room.

4 Jenna makes a 2-D picture model on a computer. Alfonso makes a 3-D diorama model. Which of the following **best** describes the difference between the two models?

Ⓕ Jenna's model shows only a view from the top of the classroom.

Ⓖ Alfonso's model shows only the floor plan of the classroom.

Ⓗ Jenna's model cannot show the placement of objects in the classroom.

Ⓘ Alfonso's model cannot show the placement of objects in the classroom.

5 Kareem has made a model of his classroom and says that in his model, the length of the classroom is twice the height of the ceiling. How could Kareem know that his statement is correct?

Ⓐ He has compared his model to another student's model.

Ⓑ He has accurately measured the length and width of the classroom.

Ⓒ He has used a meter stick to measure the height of each desk in the classroom.

Ⓓ He has taken accurate measurements of the length and height of the classroom.

Studying Science

1 Sirhan wants to make a 2-D picture model of his classroom drawn from a view that is looking down from the ceiling. Which of the following would he **not** be able to include in his model?

- (A) desks in the classroom
- (B) coat closet in the classroom
- (C) distance from the floor to the ceiling
- (D) distance from the door to the opposite wall

SC.4.N.3.1

2 A class was discussing whether to make a 2-D or 3-D model of their classroom. They listed a number of advantages and disadvantages of each. They are now debating which model to make. Which of the following is an advantage only for a 3-D model?

- (F) easy to store
- (G) takes less time to make
- (H) requires fewer tools to make the model
- (I) can show the height of objects in the room, such as a desk

SC.4.N.3.1

3 Aba is studying parts of a plant. Which tool would be **most** useful if Aba wants to see parts of a leaf?

- (A) hand lens
- (B) magnifying box
- (C) microscope
- (D) telescope

SC.4.N.1.2

4 Anna wants to compare the amounts of rainfall each month during a 4-month period. She looks at different data that her classmates recorded during that time. Which data table would Anna find **most** useful?

(F)
Month	Rainfall (cm)
March	3
April	4
May	5
June	3

(G)
Month	Days with more than 1 cm of rain
March	0
April	0
May	2
June	1

(H)
Month	Number of rainy days
March	3
April	6
May	6
June	3

(I)
Month	Hours of rainfall
March	8
Apr	9
May	12
June	15

SC.4.N.1.7

5 Brian conducted an experiment to test the strength of a packing foam material. He finds that the material gets a dent if he puts more than three bricks on it. What can Brian conclude?

- (A) The foam is not very strong.
- (B) The brick is too heavy for his test.
- (C) The foam will dent if he puts six bricks on it.
- (D) The foam will not dent if he puts five blocks of wood on it.

SC.4.N.1.4

6 Different groups of students used a ruler to measure the length of a leaf. They recorded their measurements in their science notebooks. Why should the groups show their data to one another?

(F) They are curious about what the other groups did.

(G) They want to decide which group recorded the data most neatly.

(H) They want to record all of the measurements in the same notebook.

(I) They want to compare their work and make sure they get the correct measurement.

SC.4.N.1.2

7 Logan measures the rainfall in his city each day for a month. Which of the following is an observation he could make about the amount of rainfall he observed?

(A) The rainfall kept many people from going outdoors.

(B) The amount of rainfall will decrease during the summer.

(C) The rainfall was greatest during the third week of the month.

(D) The amount of rainfall will probably be higher next month.

SC.4.N.1.7

8 Some scientists study life. Others study nonliving matter and energy. Which topic relates to Earth science?

(F) water as a source of energy

(G) water for cleaning dirty clothes

(H) water falling from clouds as rain

(I) water as a home for living organisms

SC.4.N.2.1

9 John observes that snow is dry, light, and fluffy at times. At other times, snow is wet, heavy, and sticky. John wonders what makes snow different. He wants to plan an experiment to find an answer. Why should John research his question before experimenting?

(A) to make it easier to share results

(B) to find information to help set up his experiment

(C) to decide whether the scientific method should be used

(D) to reduce the number of steps needed for the experiment

SC.4.N.1.1

10 Chad wraps three jars with three different materials: foil, cotton, and wool. Then he fills the jars with hot water of the same temperature. Chad concludes that wool is better than cotton or foil at keeping a liquid warm. What evidence would support Chad's conclusion?

(F) The final water temperature was coolest in the jar wrapped in cotton.

(G) The final water temperature was coolest in the jar wrapped in wool.

(H) The final water temperature was warmest in the jar wrapped in wool.

(I) The final water temperature was the same in the jars wrapped in cotton and foil.

SC.4.N.1.7

11 Scientists study the natural world. Evidence is an important part of their studies. What is evidence?

(A) an educated guess

(B) data that support or reject a hypothesis

(C) communicating results

(D) statement about what will happen in an experiment

SC.4.N.1.7

12 Some models have three dimensions. The dimensions are length, width, and height. Which model below has three dimensions?

(F) drawing of a skeleton

(G) photograph of a skeleton

(H) plastic model of a skeleton

(I) computer model of a skeleton shown on a monitor

SC.4.N.3.1

13 Greta makes two models of Earth's layers. She draws one model using construction paper. She uses an apple for the second model. What is **true** about these models?

(A) Both models are three-dimensional.

(B) Only the apple model can show what Earth looks like inside.

(C) Only the paper model can show where the core is located inside Earth.

(D) Both models suggest how thick each layer is compared to other layers.

SC.4.N.3.1

14 Cameron studies a model of a human heart. The heart has parts that Cameron can remove and hold in his hands before he puts the model back together. What kind of model is Cameron using?

(F) mental model

(G) computer model

(H) two-dimensional model

(I) three-dimensional model

SC.4.N.3.1

15 Dan noticed that the day got warmer between breakfast and lunch. He recorded the temperature outside his window several times.

Time (a.m.)	Temperature (°C)
9:00	22
10:00	25
11:00	27

Which of the following would be the **most** scientific way to show the data he collected?

(A) drawing a picture

(B) making a graph

(C) writing a paragraph

(D) creating a timeline

SC.4.N.1.6

16 Jacob wants to find out which cat food his cat likes best. What variable could he use in his investigation?

(F) amount of food

(G) type of cat food

(H) when he feeds his cat

(I) where he feeds his cat

SC.4.N.1.3

17 Taylor wanted to determine if watering plants makes a difference in their growth. During her investigation, she watered only one of two plants. After a few days, she noticed that the plants looked different. What science skill did Taylor use when she noticed that one of the plants was drooping?

(A) communication   (C) observation

(B) investigation   (D) prediction

 SC.4.N.1.3

18 The table below shows the finishing times of a race.

Student	Time (sec)
Ang	85.32
José	80.09
Tyler	78.89
Matthew	80.15

Which is the correct finishing order, from fastest to slowest, of the students?

(F) Ang, Matthew, Tyler, José

(G) José, Tyler, Matthew, Ang

(H) Matthew, Ang, José, Tyler

(I) Tyler, José, Matthew, Ang

 SC.4.N.1.6

19 Karina and her classmates take water samples from the same nearby pond. Then they are to take measurements of the water temperature. How can the teacher ensure that each group's results are similar?

(A) tell students to measure using the same specific tool

(B) allow students to choose from a selection of different measuring tools

(C) instruct students to complete the experiment at the same time of day

(D) give students containers made of the same material to collect the water samples

 SC.4.N.1.5

20 Four members of the track team practice the long jump. Each jumper has a friend measure the length of the jump. The measurements are recorded below:

Jumper	Distance
Ilsa	1 m
Shane	82 cm
Antonio	95 cm
Raelene	5 dm

Who jumped the farthest?

(F) Antonio   (H) Raelene

(G) Ilsa   (I) Shane

 SC.4.N.1.5

Make a Class Almanac

Materials

Paper, pencil

Procedure

1 Work in small groups to gather data about your classmates. Each group will be assigned to find out one of the following traits about the class: number of boys and girls in the class; birth month of each student; eye color of each student; hair color of each student; number of students with attached earlobes and detached earlobes; number of right-handed students and left-handed students.

2 Each group will carefully record all its data and then synthesize its findings in a graph or table. Decide what kind of graph or table is the best to show a particular set of data. Think about what kind of data can be most easily understood when organized in a table, a bar graph, a line graph, a circle graph, a line plot, or a tally sheet.

3 Collect all the graphs and tables together to make an "almanac" about the class.

Make a Class Almanac

Materials Performance Task sheet, graph paper, pencil

Time 30-45 minutes

Suggested Grouping Small groups

Inquiry Skills Record, display data, interpret data, draw conclusions

Preparation Hints Review with students the appropriate and most effective application of tables, circle graphs, line plots, bar graphs, and line graphs.

Introduce the Task Remind students that doing an investigation involves gathering data. When data is organized in a table or graph, its meaning can be understood and interpreted more easily. Also describe the kind of information typically contained in almanacs and explain that this information is often shown in tables and graphs.

Promote Discussion Challenge students to draw conclusions, based on the data in the graphs and tables, about gender ratios, common eye and hair colors, handedness, earlobe characteristics, and birthdays among the class members.

Scoring Rubric

Performance Indicators
_____ Works cooperatively with other team members.
_____ Accurately records the data that is gathered.
_____ Displays the data in a graph that is labelled correctly.
Observations and Rubric Score
3   2   1   0

How Does Earth Rotate and Revolve in Space?

1 Scientists describe Earth as having an imaginary line through it from pole to pole, about which Earth spins. What is this imaginary line called?

(A) axis

(B) equator

(C) plane

(D) satellite

2 A person living on Earth sees daytime and nighttime every 24 hr. Which of these is responsible for changes from daytime to nighttime on Earth?

(F) Earth's tilt

(G) Earth orbiting the sun

(H) moon orbiting Earth

(I) Earth rotating about its axis

3 Caroline looks up at the night sky on a clear night. She is searching for patterns of stars in the sky. What is Caroline looking for?

(A) planets

(B) galaxies

(C) constellations

(D) other planets' moons

4 Hundreds of years ago, people observed constellations in the night sky. How were constellations originally named and identified?

(F) by their brightness

(G) with latitude and longitude

(H) by their distance from Earth

(I) by the patterns they formed in the sky

5 We know that each year has four seasons: winter, spring, summer, and fall. Why do we have seasons?

(A) tilt of Earth's axis

(B) shape of Earth's orbit

(C) length of a year on Earth

(D) rotation of Earth about its axis

Name _____ Date _____

How Does Earth Move in Space?

1 Patti decided to use a basketball as a model of Earth. She placed the ball on the floor and then spun it. What was Patti demonstrating with her model of Earth?

- (A) Earth's axis
- (B) Earth's orbit
- (C) Earth's rotation
- (D) Earth's revolution

2 Earth orbits the sun. Yet the sun appears to move through the sky. For example, the sun always appears to rise in the east and set in the west. What is responsible for this apparent motion of the sun?

- (F) Earth's size
- (G) Earth's orbit
- (H) Earth's rotation
- (I) Earth's revolution

3 Earth, the sun, and the moon all rotate. The table below lists how long it takes each one to complete one rotation.

Object	Time to complete one rotation
Earth	About 24 hr
moon	About 27 days
sun	About 27 days

What can you conclude from the data in this table?

- (A) The moon spins faster than the sun.
- (B) The sun spins faster than the moon.
- (C) Both the sun and moon spin faster than Earth.
- (D) Both the sun and moon spin more slowly than Earth.

4 While Earth revolves around the sun, Earth is also rotating. About how many rotations does Earth complete as it orbits once around the sun?

- (F) 1
- (G) 7
- (H) 30
- (I) 365

5 Scientists use models to represent or explain things in the natural world. Why are models useful for the study of the movements of the sun, the moon, and Earth?

- (A) Models cannot be proved wrong.
- (B) Models are always accepted by all scientists.
- (C) Models describe the way things actually are.
- (D) Models can be used to make testable predictions.

What Are Moon Phases?

1 Earth is a planet in the solar system. A planet can have one or more moons. What is another word that means the same as moon?

(A) asteroid

(B) comet

(C) satellite

(D) star

2 Kashvi likes to look out the window at the moon. She observes that it seems to change every week. Which sentence **best** explains why this happens?

(F) The moon moves between Earth and the sun.

(G) The moon rotates only once in about a month.

(H) The same side of the moon always faces Earth.

(I) The amount of the lighted part of the moon that faces Earth changes.

3 People on Earth see the moon every night. Sometimes people also see the moon during the day. Why does this happen?

(A) The moon makes its own light.

(B) The moon moves closer to Earth.

(C) The moon is reflecting light from Earth.

(D) The moon is reflecting light from the sun.

4 From space, the surfaces of Earth and the moon look different. How is the surface of the moon different from the surface of Earth?

(F) no air, no liquid water, craters and mountains, rocky

(G) air, no liquid water, craters and mountains, not rocky

(H) air, liquid water, craters and mountains, not rocky

(I) air, liquid water, no craters or mountains, rocky

5 One kind of modern calendar is a lunar calendar. What is a lunar calendar based on?

(A) phases of the moon

(B) yearly cycle of the sun

(C) monthly phases of the sun

(D) daily rising and setting of the moon

How Does Technology Help Us Learn About Space?

1 Jamil is writing a report about Galileo's telescope. What should he say was the **main idea** that Galileo proved with the telescope?

- (A) how close Earth is to the moon
- (B) that the sun is the center of the solar system
- (C) that the moon circles around Earth each month
- (D) how long it takes Earth to circle around the sun

2 Adam is reading a story about the possibility of a first close encounter people might have with another planet. Which of the following would **most** likely be responsible for this encounter?

- (F) space antenna
- (G) space probe
- (H) space shuttle
- (I) space station

3 Ming wrote the following statements on the board about space shuttles. Which is **not** a true statement?

- (A) It orbits Earth.
- (B) It can be reused.
- (C) It carries astronauts to the moon.
- (D) It brings supplies to the space station.

4 Tashon is making a class display about the Russian spacecraft *Sputnik 1*, the first satellite to orbit Earth in 1957. Why was the launch of this spacecraft so important?

- (F) It was the first to visit another planet.
- (G) It was first to carry a person into space.
- (H) It carried the first space station into orbit.
- (I) It increased people's interest in space exploration.

5 Denzel visited Kennedy Space Center. Many other people were visiting there, too. How does a high number of visitors to the space center **most** help Florida?

- (A) People get to meet the astronauts.
- (B) Many people get to see the shuttle.
- (C) More people get to visit the beaches.
- (D) Visitors bring more money into the state.

Earth's Place in Space

Unit Benchmark Test

❶ The motions of Earth, the sun, and the moon can be shown with simple diagrams. For example, look closely at the following diagram.

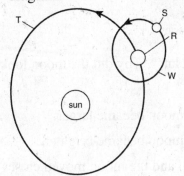

Which letter represents the motion that takes about 28 days?

Ⓐ R

Ⓑ S

Ⓒ T

Ⓓ W

SC.4.E.5.3, SC.4.N.3.1

❷ Luis wanted to build a model of how Earth and the moon revolve and rotate. Which table below shows the **best** models Luis can use for Earth, the moon, and the sun?

Ⓕ

Body	Model
Earth	Golf ball
moon	Soccer ball
sun	Baseball

Ⓖ

Body	Model
Earth	Baseball
moon	Soccer ball
sun	Golf ball

Ⓗ

Body	Model
Earth	Soccer ball
moon	Golf ball
sun	Baseball

Ⓘ

Body	Model
Earth	Baseball
moon	Golf ball
sun	Soccer ball

SC.4.E.5.4, SC.4.N.3.1

❸ Earth spins at a very constant and regular speed. How long does it take for Earth to make one complete rotation?

Ⓐ 24 hr

Ⓑ 24 days

Ⓒ 365 hr

Ⓓ 365 days

SC.4.E.5.4

❹ The sun appears to move across the sky during the day. Why does this happen?

Ⓕ Earth's tilt on its axis

Ⓖ moon orbiting Earth

Ⓗ Earth's rotation on its axis

Ⓘ Earth's orbit around the sun

SC.4.E.5.4

❺ When we say something is in orbit, we mean that it is traveling around another object in space. Which of the following does Earth orbit?

Ⓐ sun

Ⓑ moon

Ⓒ Mars

Ⓓ Venus

SC.4.E.5.3

❻ Earth's movement around the sun happens at a very constant rate. What would happen if Earth took longer to travel around the sun than it does now?

Ⓕ Earth would be hotter.

Ⓖ The seasons would be shorter.

Ⓗ A day would be shorter than 24 hr.

Ⓘ A year would be longer than 365 days.

SC.4.E.5.3

7 The data table below shows how long it takes each inner planet to make one complete rotation and revolution. The numbers listed are in Earth days (24-hour periods).

Planet	Time needed to make one complete rotation (Earth days)	Time needed to make one complete revolution (Earth days)
Mercury	58.6	87.96
Venus	243	224.7
Earth	1	365.26
Mars	1.02	687

According to the data table, which statement is **correct**?

Ⓐ Venus's orbit is the shortest of the inner planets.

Ⓑ Mercury's orbit is the longest of the inner planets.

Ⓒ Earth completes one full rotation faster than any other inner planet.

Ⓓ Earth's rotation time is closest to that of Venus.

 SC.4.E.5.4

8 The picture below shows a phase of the moon.

What will the **next** phase be?

Ⓕ new moon

Ⓖ first quarter

Ⓗ last quarter

Ⓘ full moon

SC.4.E.5.2

9 Emily saw the moon one night. It looked like the picture below.

New moon

One week later, why did the moon look bigger?

Ⓐ The moon became larger.

Ⓑ The moon became brighter.

Ⓒ Earth and the moon moved closer together.

Ⓓ Emily could see more of the side of the moon that was lit.

SC.4.E.5.2

10 The moon revolves around Earth. How long does the moon take to revolve once?

Ⓕ about as long as Earth's seasons

Ⓖ about as long as one rotation of Earth

Ⓗ about as long as one rotation of the moon

Ⓘ about as long as one revolution of Earth around the sun

SC.4.E.5.2

11 When Andrew looks at the moon at night, it appears to be shining. Why does the moon look this way?

Ⓐ It makes its own light.

Ⓑ It reflects light from Earth.

Ⓒ It reflects light from the sun.

Ⓓ It reflects light from the other planets.

SC.4.E.5.2

Name _____ Date _____

12 The picture below shows a phase of the moon.

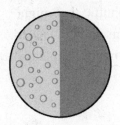

Which phase is it?

- (F) full moon
- (G) new moon
- (H) third quarter
- (I) waning crescent

SC.4.E.5.2

13 Both lunar and solar calendars are divided into months. The timeline below shows both kinds of months.

Solar months

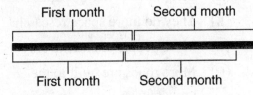

Lunar months

Which of the following describes a lunar month?

- (A) half as long as a solar month
- (B) twice as long as a solar month
- (C) the same length as a solar month
- (D) a little shorter than a solar month

SC.4.E.5.2

14 Refracting telescopes were the first type of telescopes used by astronomers. The world's largest refracting telescope is located in Wisconsin and was built in 1897.

Which of the following is an example of something you could see with this instrument?

- (F) inside of a leaf
- (G) surface of the moon
- (H) bright light from the sun
- (I) minerals that make up a rock

SC.4.E.6.5

15 Hahn's school project is about communication satellites that are carried into space by the space shuttles. The picture shows one type of satellite.

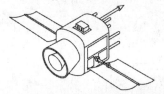

The flat panels on the side of the satellite absorb light energy from the sun. Which similar type of technology is used by people on Earth?

- (A) television screens
- (B) computer monitors
- (C) blades on windmills
- (D) solar cells on houses

SC.4.E.6.5

16 Ling's family is camping in the forest. The picture below shows their campsite.

Zippered sleeping bag

Waterproof tent

Canteen

Freeze-dried food

Space blanket

Backpack

Flashlight

Which of these supplies was first developed for the space program?

(F) waterproof tent

(G) battery flashlight

(H) freeze-dried food

(I) zipppered sleeping bag

SC.4.E.6.5

17 Rana's class is studying space exploration. The students will learn that the development of which technology was **most** important before space exploration could begin?

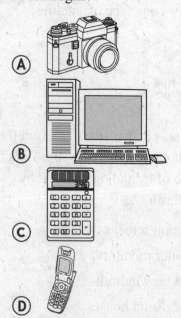

(A)

(B)

(C)

(D)

SC.4.E.6.5

18 When a space shuttle takes off, NASA scientists use an infrared camera to look for hot areas in the shuttle that might signal a problem. This camera is also used by which of the following people on Earth?

(F) doctors

(G) firefighters

(H) building engineers

(I) restaurant managers

SC.4.E.6.5

19 Jamal's class is making a list of ways that the space program has affected Florida. Which of the following is the **most** important way that having the space program in Florida has helped Florida universities?

(A) They have better buildings.

(B) They do more space research.

(C) More people attend the universities.

(D) More roads are built to the universities.

SC.4.E.5.5

20 The *Skylab* space station had a device that warned NASA if there were any dangerous vapors in the air. What technology in homes now uses this technology?

(F) light bulb

(G) computer

(H) air conditioner

(I) smoke detector

SC.4.E.6.5

Name _____ Date _____

It's Just a Phase!

Materials

lamp without a shade

softball or baseball

Procedure

With your group, you are going to model the phases of the moon, using a lamp without a shade and a small ball.

❶ When the teacher darkens the room, turn on the lamp.

❷ Begin by standing with your back to the lamp.

❸ Hold the ball at arm's length in front of you, but above the level of your head. Make sure the ball is in the light.

❹ Rotate counterclockwise, keeping the ball in the same position relative to you as it revolves. Stop each eighth of the way around, and draw a picture that shows how much of the ball appears lighted.

❺ What does the lamp represent? What does the ball represent?

_____

❻ Describe how much of the lighted half of the ball you could see and your position at each stopping point in your rotation. What is each similar phase of the moon called?

_____

_____

❼ Explain what causes the phases of the moon.

_____

_____

It's Just a Phase!

Materials Performance Task sheet, lamp without a shade, softball or baseball

Time 30 minutes

Suggested Grouping groups of three

Inquiry Skills use models, observe, compare

Preparation Hints none

Introduce the Task Tell students that they will be modeling the phases of the moon. One student in each group will move the ball, and the other two will draw what is happening. Students should answer questions on the Performance Task sheet individually, after a small-group discussion.

Promote Discussion When students finish, ask why it was important to hold the ball above the level of the head. (to keep it in the light; to prevent the person's shadow from falling on the ball)

Scoring Rubric

Performance Indicators
_____ Works with the group to model the phases of the moon according to directions.
_____ Works with the group to create drawings of the moon's cycle.
_____ Can identify and name the phases of the moon.
_____ Clearly explains the phases of the moon's cycle.

Observations and Rubric Score
3   2   1   0

How Do Weathering and Erosion Shape Earth's Surface?

1 The water in a fast-moving river causes rocks to bump and scrape against one another. What will happen to these rocks over time?

(A) They will get larger.

(B) They will get smaller.

(C) They will get sharper.

(D) They will get heavier.

2 Ms. Estrada asks her science class to design an activity that will make rocks smooth like the ones they find near the river. Which activity shows how a river makes rocks smooth?

(F) Place the rocks in direct sunlight.

(G) Bury the rocks in soil under water.

(H) Put the rocks under a heavy weight.

(I) Shake the rocks in a container of water.

3 There is a relationship between landforms and the movement of water. Given this relationship, which of the following landforms is the result of weathering?

(A) canyon

(B) desert

(C) forest

(D) mountain

4 Wind, like water, can cause erosion. Which of the following choices is an example of wind erosion?

(F) alluvial fan

(G) moraine

(H) sand dunes

(I) tides

5 The movement of water can cause erosion. Which of the following choices is a result of water erosion?

(A) barrier islands

(B) canyons

(C) small rocks

(D) smooth stones

What Are Minerals?

1 Minerals can be sorted based on their hardness. The Mohs' scale lists the hardness of specific minerals. Which statement **best** explains how scientists use the Mohs' scale to help them determine a mineral's hardness?

Ⓐ No two minerals have the same hardness.

Ⓑ Minerals with the same hardness are usually the same color.

Ⓒ A mineral can scratch another mineral only if it has a lower hardness.

Ⓓ Minerals will scratch other minerals only if they have the same hardness.

2 There are several ways that minerals are made. Which mineral can form when a large pool of seawater slowly evaporates?

Ⓕ apatite

Ⓖ halite

Ⓗ mica

Ⓘ quartz

3 Paolo wanted to identify a mineral. He rubbed a corner of the mineral across a white tile and recorded the color of the mark. What property was Paolo measuring?

Ⓐ cleavage

Ⓑ color

Ⓒ luster

Ⓓ streak

4 The Mohs' scale lists diamond as the hardest mineral. What does this mean?

Ⓕ Diamonds can scratch any other material.

Ⓖ Diamonds weigh more for a given size than any other mineral.

Ⓗ Diamond is the only mineral that does not leave a streak on a tile plate.

Ⓘ Diamond is the only mineral that will not break when hit with a hammer.

5 Minerals can be identified by their hardness. What is the hardest mineral?

Ⓐ corundum

Ⓑ diamond

Ⓒ quartz

Ⓓ talc

What Are Properties of Minerals?

❶ Bethany and Ian are each given a sample of the mineral quartz and asked to compare their samples. Bethany is given a sample of smoky quartz, and Ian is given a sample of rose quartz. Which property is **least likely** to be the same for the two samples?

- Ⓐ cleavage
- Ⓑ color
- Ⓒ hardness
- Ⓓ streak

❷ Jorge is studying a sample of the mineral galena. He describes the galena as cubic, gray, metallic, and opaque. Which term describes galena's luster?

- Ⓕ cubic
- Ⓖ gray
- Ⓗ metallic
- Ⓘ opaque

❸ A group of students was given samples of three unknown minerals. The table below shows the observations they recorded.

Sample	Color	Streak color
1	brown	red
2	red	red
3	brown	blue

Which samples are **most likely** to be the same mineral?

- Ⓐ 1 and 2 only
- Ⓑ 1 and 3 only
- Ⓒ 2 and 3 only
- Ⓓ 1, 2, and 3

❹ On a school trip, Chan is looking for mineral samples on a beach. Chan records all the physical properties of the mineral he can identify just by looking at and touching each mineral. Which property would Chan **least likely** be able to identify?

- Ⓕ color
- Ⓖ hardness
- Ⓗ luster
- Ⓘ texture

❺ Donna has two rocks that she thinks are the same mineral. She decides to conduct a streak test to compare them. She runs each mineral along a streak plate, which leaves a line of powder on the plate. What should Donna observe to compare the rocks?

- Ⓐ whether the powder is dull or shiny
- Ⓑ whether the rock scratched the plate
- Ⓒ the color of the line on the plate
- Ⓓ the shape of the powder crystals

How Can Rocks Be Classified?

1 In science class, Caleb learns that in the rock cycle, rocks change from one form to another. Weathering is one of the forces in the rock cycle. Which of these events is an example of weathering?

Ⓐ eruption of lava that cools quickly on the side of a volcano

Ⓑ magma that explodes onto Earth's surface

Ⓒ limestone that changes into marble

Ⓓ shale that wears away over time

2 Miners can find different kinds of metal in different types of rocks. The metal can be used for making tools, cooking utensils, and jewelry. Which of these is a metal that can be mined from rocks?

Ⓕ coal

Ⓖ copper

Ⓗ pumice

Ⓘ schist

3 Sheila is classifying the rocks in her collection. She knows that limestone often contains fossils. In which category of rock should she classify these rocks?

Ⓐ igneous

Ⓑ granite

Ⓒ metamorphic

Ⓓ sedimentary

4 Karen's mom buys a pumice stone at the store. She uses it to smooth rough patches of skin on her feet. She accidentally dropped the pumice in her bath water and was surprised to see the stone float. Why does this kind of rock float?

Ⓕ It is formed from quartz sands.

Ⓖ It contains sediment from fish scales.

Ⓗ It is a rock that has lots of gas bubbles or air-filled chambers in it.

Ⓘ It is a metamorphic rock that is very lightweight.

5 May Ling is examining a piece of limestone with a hand lens. She knows that sedimentary rock has many properties. Which is a property of sedimentary rock?

Ⓐ It contains no minerals.

Ⓑ It is made of many layers.

Ⓒ It is made from magma or cooled lava.

Ⓓ It is made from the bacteria of live and dead plants.

What Resources Are Found in Florida?

1 Water is an important resource in Florida. Freshwater is used for homes and businesses. Salt water is used for recreation and fishing. What type of resource is water?

(A) human resource

(B) mineral resource

(C) renewable resource

(D) nonrenewable resource

2 Devin's family is building a house. His parents want to use a renewable energy source to provide energy for the house. Which of the following could they use?

(F) coal

(G) natural gas

(H) oil

(I) solar energy

3 Silica is an important resource found in Florida. What is one way that people use silica?

(A) to make solar panels

(B) to build houses

(C) to produce electricity

(D) as a gemstone in jewelry

4 Benjamin's family lives on a farm in Florida. The photograph shows how the farm produces some of its electricity.

Based on the photograph, what type of resource is Benjamin's family using?

(F) new

(G) nonrenewable

(H) recyclable

(I) renewable

5 Air pollution is a common problem in Florida. It is often caused by burning fossil fuels. Which of these is a renewable source of energy that causes less air pollution?

(A) coal

(B) gas

(C) oil

(D) sunlight

Rocks, Minerals, and Resources

1 Antonio is getting ready for school. What type of resource does Antonio use along with his toothbrush and toothpaste when he is ready to brush his teeth?

- (A) fossil
- (C) nonrenewable
- (B) new
- (D) renewable

SC.4.E.6.3

2 Brian is washing dishes after breakfast. What should Brian do to conserve water while he is washing dishes?

- (F) Turn off the water until it is time to rinse.
- (G) Use a soft sponge to wash the dishes.
- (H) Use cold water to wash and hot water to rinse.
- (I) Ask someone to dry the dishes after he washes them.

SC.4.E.6.3

3 Florida's nickname is the Sunshine State. Sunshine is one of Florida's most abundant resources. What type of resource is sunshine?

- (A) fossil
- (C) renewable
- (B) nonrenewable
- (D) scarce

SC.4.E.6.3

4 Tamika goes hiking and sees an interesting rock formation. The formation looks like it has many different layers. What category of rock did she find?

- (F) conglomerate
- (H) metamorphic
- (G) igneous
- (I) sedimentary

SC.4.E.6.1

5 Chloe often tells her brother to turn off the lights in their home. She tells him it is important to conserve energy. Why is it important to conserve energy?

- (A) Energy cannot be purchased in small amounts.
- (B) Energy most often comes from renewable resources.
- (C) Energy most often comes from nonrenewable resources.
- (D) Energy is very difficult to bring into the home.

SC.4.E.6.3

6 One of Florida's most abundant resources can be collected and turned into electricity for homes and businesses.

Which Florida resource is being collected in this picture?

- (F) solar energy
- (G) wave energy
- (H) wind energy
- (I) water energy

SC.4.E.6.6

7 Water is a renewable resource found in Florida. The state is surrounded on three sides by the Atlantic Ocean and the Gulf of Mexico. It is also home to many inland freshwater lakes and rivers. What makes water a renewable resource?

(A) It does not cause pollution.

(B) It is constantly recycled so it can be used again.

(C) It is necessary for all plants and animals to live.

(D) It takes hundreds of years for water to be created after it is used.

SC.4.E.6.3

8 Minerals and rocks are not exactly the same. How are minerals and rocks related to each other?

(F) Minerals are groups of related rocks.

(G) Minerals have crystals, but rocks do not.

(H) Rocks are made up of one or more minerals.

(I) Rocks contain different chemical compounds than minerals.

SC.4.E.6.2

9 A new library is being built, and the builders are using stone for the steps at the library entrance. They want to use a hard, strong rock that will not break easily or erode. Which of these rocks might work well for making strong, lasting steps?

(A) chalk   (C) marble

(B) limestone   (D) shale

SC.4.E.6.1

10 A group of students identified some mineral samples and used the table below to display their findings. During their investigation, one mineral caused a compass needle to turn away from North.

Mineral	Luster	Streak	Other characteristics
calcite	glassy	white	bubbles when cold dilute hydrochloric acid is dropped on it
graphite	metallic	black	feels greasy
magnetite	metallic	black	magnetic
mica	nonmetallic	none	peels into thin flakes
talc	nonmetallic	white to very pale green	feels greasy

What was the mineral?

(F) calcite   (H) magnetite

(G) graphite   (I) mica

SC.4.E.6.2

11 The mineral below is soft enough to scratch with your fingernail. It is made up of many thin sheets that can be pulled apart into large flakes.

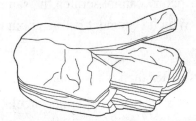

What mineral is shown?

(A) diamond   (C) mica

(B) gold   (D) quartz

SC.4.E.6.2

12 You have a colorless mineral that you want to identify. You cannot scratch the mineral with your fingernail, which has a hardness of about 2.5, but you can scratch it with a steel nail. The hardness of a steel nail is about 5.5.

Mineral	Hardness	Streak	Color
gold	2.5 to 3	yellow	yellow
calcite	3	white	colorless or white
hematite	5.5 to 6.5	reddish-brown	silver-gray or red
feldspar	6	none	colorless or pink
pyrite	6 to 6.5	greenish-black	yellow
quartz	7	none	colorless, pink, brown, and many other colors

Based on the information in the table, which mineral could your sample be?

(F) calcite
(G) feldspar
(H) hematite
(I) quartz

SC.4.E.6.2

13 A steel nail can scratch a certain mineral. A copper penny cannot scratch the same mineral. Which statement is true about the mineral?

(A) It is softer than copper and steel.
(B) It is harder than copper and steel.
(C) It is harder than steel, but softer than copper.
(D) It is harder than copper, but softer than steel.

SC.4.E.6.2, SC.4.N.1.1

14 Look at the illustration. Long ago, this creature was caught in muck, a slimy mud, on a sea floor before it turned to rock.

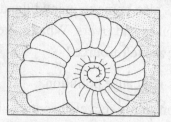

Which of these words tells what this item is today?

(F) fossil
(G) layer
(H) outcrop
(I) shell

SC.4.E.6.1

15 The action of ocean waves and currents can change Earth's surface. Which of the following landforms is created by ocean waves and currents?

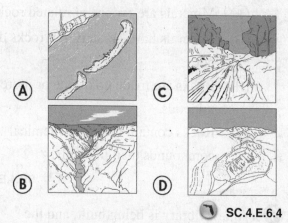

(A)
(B)
(C)
(D)

SC.4.E.6.4

16 Erosion and weathering are different processes that involve some of the same agents, such as wind, water, and ice. How is erosion different from weathering?

(F) Erosion is slower than weathering.

(G) Erosion is faster than weathering.

(H) Erosion breaks rocks and weathering moves rocks.

(I) Erosion moves rocks and weathering breaks rocks.

SC.4.E.6.4

17 Zack studies the categories of rocks during science class. He knows that not all kinds of rock are formed in the same way. He sees this illustration on a worksheet.

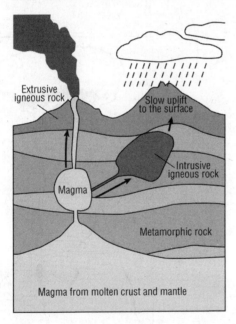

What title should Zack put on this illustration?

(A) weathering

(B) the complete rock cycle

(C) how igneous rock is formed

(D) how metamorphic rock is formed

SC.4.E.6.1

18 What kind of landform forms on a beach and is caused by wind erosion?

(F) landslide   (H) moraine

(G) sand dune   (I) sinkhole

SC.4.E.6.4

19 Many rocks contain gaps or cracks. In the diagram below, notice the relationship between the rock and the plant.

Which statement describes what will happen to the rock and the plant over time?

(A) The rock will crush the plant.

(B) The plant will be buried in the crack.

(C) The plant will grow, and the crack will get bigger.

(D) The rock will stop the plant from growing bigger.

SC.4.E.6.4

20 If you look closely at beach sand, you will see that it is made up of tiny rocks and other materials. How is this sand on an ocean beach formed?

(F) Alluvial fans create the sand.

(G) Waves weather rocks and shells.

(H) Wind blows sand from nearby deserts.

(I) Landslides bring sand down from cliffs.

SC.4.E.6.4

Weathering and Erosion

Materials

poster board

pencil

colored markers

research materials

Procedure

❶ Show how weathering and erosion affect rocks. Use what you have learned in this chapter. Also use research materials that you find in your classroom or in the media center.

❷ On the poster board, draw pictures of how weathering and erosion affect rocks. Use a pencil to draw, and then color your picture with markers.

❸ Share your poster with the class. Explain how weathering and erosion caused the changes shown on your poster.

Weathering and Erosion

Materials Performance Task sheet, poster board, pencil, colored markers, research material

Time 30–45 minutes (You may wish to allow students some time before the project to review the chapter and research weathering and erosion in the media center.)

Suggested Grouping small groups

Inquiry Skills display data, communicate

Preparation Hints You may choose to provide magazines for finding pictures to illustrate weathering and erosion. You and your students may find many other materials to illustrate weathering and erosion.

Introduce the Task Review the topics of weathering and erosion with the class before breaking into small groups. Allow time for students to brainstorm how they will complete the task.

Promote Discussion When students have finished, allow time for each group to share its poster. Encourage students to describe how weathering and erosion caused the changes depicted on their posters.

Scoring Rubric

Performance Indicators

_____ Uses research skills to organize information.

_____ Reveals an understanding of the concepts of weathering and erosion.

_____ Assembles illustrations to show how weathering and erosion affect rock.

_____ Communicates findings effectively.

Observations and Rubric Score

3   2   1   0

Name _____ Date _____

What Are Physical Properties of Matter?

1 All matter has certain properties. Which of the following can be classified as matter?

   (A) the number 25

   (B) a dream

   (C) the day Monday

   (D) a puddle of water

2 Kaleesha says that taste is not a property of matter. Which statement below **best** describes why Kaleesha is not correct?

   (F) Taste does not have mass.

   (G) Taste has a density less than water.

   (H) You cannot measure the volume of taste.

   (I) Taste is a physical property that can be described.

3 Maxim wants to measure the volume of a brick. Which instrument should he choose to measure the volume?

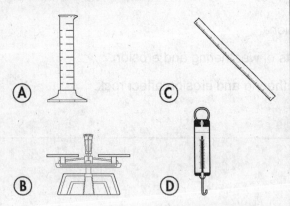

4 Darlene places a small cube of wood into a beaker filled with water. The wood floats on top of the water. Which of these **best** explains why the wood block floats?

   (F) Most objects will float on water.

   (G) The wood block has less mass than the water.

   (H) The water has more volume than the wood block.

   (I) The wood block has a density that is less than that of water.

5 Kaylie is describing the physical properties of an orange and a lemon. Which two physical properties can she determine without using any measurement instruments?

   (A) mass and color

   (B) texture and volume

   (C) odor and taste

   (D) shape and density

How Are Physical Properties Observed?

1 Objects can be sorted into groups using properties. What is a physical property of an object?

(A) the number of different objects in a group

(B) the name of the person who owns the object

(C) the distance between a person and the object

(D) something that can be observed about the object

2 Length is another physical property that can be observed. The picture below demonstrates one way to find length.

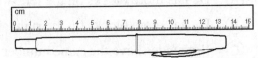

What is the length of the pen?

(F) 12.8 cm

(G) 13 cm

(H) 13.5 cm

(I) 14 cm

3 During science class, the teacher displayed a glass containing a liquid. The teacher said the liquid was either water or colorless vinegar. What physical property could the students use to identify that the liquid is vinegar?

(A) color

(B) mass

(C) smell

(D) volume

4 Objects can be sorted using physical properties that can be measured. What property of an object can be measured using a pan balance?

(F) hardness

(G) length

(H) mass

(I) volume

5 Dottie has a blue plastic set of alphabet letters. She decides to sort the letters using a physical property. Which property should she use?

(A) color

(B) hardness

(C) odor

(D) shape

What Is Conservation of Mass?

❶ Suzanne makes a tower out of six identical plastic blocks. Then she uses a pan balance to measure the mass of the tower. She finds that the tower's mass is 72 g. What is the mass of each block?

Ⓐ 10 g   Ⓒ 36 g

Ⓑ 12 g   Ⓓ 66 g

❷ Caleb has two identical rubber band airplanes. He puts one airplane on one pan of a balance. He takes the other airplane apart and places the parts on the other pan of the balance. What will he **most likely** observe about the pans of the balance?

Ⓕ The pan with the airplane will be even with the pan with the parts.

Ⓖ The pan with the airplane will be slightly lower than the pan with the parts.

Ⓗ The pan with the airplane will be slightly higher than the pan with the parts.

Ⓘ The pan with the airplane will be completely lowered, and the pan with the parts will be completely raised.

❸ Ben uses a balance to measure the mass of some snap-together blocks. The mass of a red block is 3 g, a blue block is 5 g, and a yellow block is 7 g. He then makes a toy building using three of each type of block. If he measures the mass of the building, what would it **most likely** be?

Ⓐ 44 g   Ⓒ 46 g

Ⓑ 45 g   Ⓓ 49 g

❹ Ammon puts seven identical blocks on a balance. He finds that their total mass is 42 g. He then removes three blocks and measures the remaining mass. What **most likely** is the mass of the remaining blocks?

Ⓕ 18 g   Ⓗ 28 g

Ⓖ 24 g   Ⓘ 32 g

❺ Joshua has a bag of identical blocks. He makes a toy building using 15 of the blocks and puts it on the left side of a balance. He puts a handful of blocks on the right side of the balance. The right side sinks down. Why does this **most likely** happen?

Ⓐ He has more blocks on the left side.

Ⓑ He has more blocks on the right side.

Ⓒ Both sides have the same number of blocks, but combining them adds slightly to the mass.

Ⓓ Both sides have the same number of blocks, but combining them takes away slightly from the mass.

Name _____ Date _____

What Are the States of Water?

❶ The three states of matter are solid, liquid, and gas. Which process changes water vapor into liquid water?

Ⓐ condensation
Ⓑ evaporation
Ⓒ freezing
Ⓓ melting

❷ Saqib placed an ice cube on a plate. The ice cube changed from a solid to a liquid. What happened to the amount of matter in the ice cube?

Ⓕ It doubled.
Ⓖ It tripled.
Ⓗ It stayed the same.
Ⓘ It decreased slightly.

❸ Jose has a pot full of water. He knows that water can change states when energy is added or removed. Which of the following actions would add energy to the pot of water?

Ⓐ heating the water on the stove
Ⓑ placing the water in the freezer
Ⓒ leaving the water outside on a cold night
Ⓓ pouring the water into a larger container

❹ Water changes states when energy is added or taken away. What happens to water vapor when energy is taken away?

Ⓕ It melts into a solid.
Ⓖ It freezes into a liquid.
Ⓗ It condenses into a liquid.
Ⓘ It evaporates into a solid.

❺ Water is matter. All matter is made of particles. Which statement best describes how water particles are arranged in different states of matter?

Ⓐ The particles in a gas are farther apart than the particles in a solid.
Ⓑ The particles in a gas are closer together than the particles in a solid.
Ⓒ The particles in a solid are farther apart than the particles in a liquid.
Ⓓ The particles in a gas are closer together than the particles in a liquid.

What Are Magnets?

❶ A few materials are magnetic, but most are not. If an object is attracted to a magnet, what is the object made of?

   Ⓐ cardboard

   Ⓑ metal

   Ⓒ plastic

   Ⓓ wood

❷ Paper clips are attracted to magnets. What property of paper clips does this illustrate?

   Ⓕ physical property

   Ⓖ chemical property

   Ⓗ geological property

   Ⓘ biological property

❸ Tiffany needs to bring an example of a magnetic object to class. She considers a few items around her house. Which of the following will she decide is attracted to a magnet?

   Ⓐ gold ring

   Ⓑ iron nail

   Ⓒ glass vase

   Ⓓ cotton T-shirt

❹ A magnet can be made by wrapping wire into a coil and passing an electric current through it. What is the name for this type of magnet?

   Ⓕ dry cell

   Ⓖ generator

   Ⓗ bar magnet

   Ⓘ electromagnet

❺ Magnets generate an invisible region in which magnetic forces act. What is the name for this region around the magnet that can attract materials?

   Ⓐ bar

   Ⓑ cell

   Ⓒ field

   Ⓓ pole

Name _____ Date _____

Unit 4

How Do Magnets Attract Objects?

Lesson 6 Quiz

1 Alexa has two different magnets. She wants to test which magnet is stronger. What could she do?

(A) See if the magnets will attract each other.

(B) See which magnet will attract a block of wood.

(C) See which magnet will attract a nail from the farthest distance.

(D) Pick a different group of objects for each magnet and see which magnet attracts the most objects.

2 Marisa helps her father make dinner. When Marisa opens the refrigerator to get some lettuce, she notices the refrigerator door has a magnetic strip that holds it closed. Why does the steel fork Marisa is holding stick to the magnetic strip on the refrigerator?

(F) The fork is also a magnet.

(G) The fork is repelled by the magnet.

(H) The fork is attracted by the magnet.

(I) The fork is attracted by the cold temperature.

3 Amari strokes a paper clip with a bar magnet 30 times. The paper clip now attracts items made of iron and steel. What happened to the paper clip?

(A) The paper clip became soft.

(B) The paper clip became cold.

(C) The paper clip became shiny.

(D) The paper clip became a magnet.

4 Kofi wants to know how two magnets behave when they are together. She knows that like poles repel each other. The magnets below show her experiment.

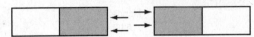

What must be **true** of the magnets shown?

(F) The two poles are the same.

(G) The two poles are opposites, south and north.

(H) The two poles are opposites, north and south.

(I) It is not possible to tell anything about the magnets.

5 James uses a tool that has a large magnet attached to a long handle and wheels. He can push the tool over sand, dirt, and grass. If an object is attracted to the magnet, what could the object contain?

(A) iron

(B) wood

(C) plastic

(D) cardboard

Matter and Its Properties

1 Smith Elementary installs a new system for students to use to buy their school lunches. Each student receives a card like the one shown below.

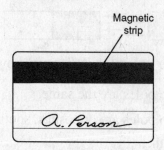

Magnetic strip

What must be true about the material in the card reader at the lunch counter?

(A) The card reader has plastic inside that reads the magnetic strip.

(B) The card reader has wood inside that reads the magnetic strip.

(C) The card reader has glass inside that reads the magnetic strip.

(D) The card reader has material with iron or steel that reads the magnetic strip.

SC.4.P.8.4, SC.4.N.1.4

2 Cora observes some items in her science kit. When she moves a stone, a paper clip in the kit moves toward the stone. Which type of force causes the paper clip to move toward the stone?

(F) a magnetic force attracting metal

(G) the sun lighting items near Earth

(H) friction acting on objects that are moving

(I) a magnetic force causing like poles to repel

SC.4.P.8.4, SC.4.N.1.4

3 Look at the image of the magnet below.

What are the ends of a magnet called?

(A) bars   (C) motors

(B) fields   (D) poles

SC.4.P.8.4

4 Bar magnets and electromagnets have similarities and differences. Which of these correctly describes one difference between bar magnets and electromagnets?

(F) Bar magnets have a magnetic field, but electromagnets do not.

(G) Electromagnets are temporary, but bar magnets are permanent.

(H) Electromagnets have two poles, but bar magnets have only one pole.

(I) Bar magnets have two poles, but electromagnets have only one pole.

SC.4.P.8.4

5 A magnet and a paper clip are on a desk. What distance between the magnet and the paper clip would result in the strongest magnetic attraction?

(A) 2 cm   (C) 7 cm

(B) 4 cm   (D) 9 cm

SC.4.P.8.4

6 Sydney's grandfather has a pacemaker in his chest to help keep his heart beating regularly. He is supposed to avoid magnetic fields that might interfere with the way his pacemaker works. Which of the following should he be careful to avoid?

(F) watching TV

(G) being near a large electric motor

(H) using an electric blanket

(I) talking on his household phone, which is not a cell phone

SC.4.P.8.4

7 On a camping trip, Bryan notices that the needle of a compass always points north to south. Why does this happen?

(A) The needle points toward colder places.

(B) Gravity makes the needle point this way.

(C) The sun makes the needle point this way.

(D) Earth has a magnetic field and the needle is magnetic.

SC.4.P.8.4

8 Cara places a group of objects on her desk. She wants to describe the objects in terms of a single property.

 Marble Horseshoe

 Rough rock Key

Which physical property is similar for all of these objects?

(F) shape

(G) texture

(H) hardness

(I) attraction to magnets

SC.4.P.8.1

9 Mariano wants to measure the volume of a 2-cm cube. What are two instruments that he could use to find the volume of the cube?

(A) ruler and spring scale

(B) pan balance and ruler

(C) ruler and graduated cylinder

(D) graduated cylinder and spring scale

SC.4.P.8.1

10 Dale has a comic book, a notebook, a writing pad, and a CD. Which of these items would **not** belong in the group if Dale classifies them by the physical property of shape?

(F) CD   (H) notebook

(G) comic book   (I) writing pad

SC.4.P.8.1

⑪ The three states of matter are solid, liquid, and gas. Which is an example of water as a solid?

Ⓐ

Ⓑ

Ⓒ

Ⓓ

SC.4.P.8.2

⑫ Water changes states when energy is added or taken away. What happens to liquid water when energy is added?

Ⓕ It melts into a gas.

Ⓖ It freezes into a solid.

Ⓗ It evaporates into a gas.

Ⓘ It condenses into a solid.

SC.4.P.8.2

⑬ Water is found as a liquid, solid, or gas. What happens when water changes from a gas to a liquid?

Ⓐ It melts.   Ⓒ It condenses.

Ⓑ It freezes.   Ⓓ It evaporates.

SC.4.P.8.2

⑭ Isamar changed water from a liquid to a gas. What did Isamar do to the water?

Ⓕ She froze the water.

Ⓖ She melted the water.

Ⓗ She added energy to the water.

Ⓘ She removed energy from the water.

SC.4.P.8.2

⑮ Water is found in all three states of matter. Which shows the change of state involved when water freezes?

Ⓐ changes from a solid into a gas

Ⓑ changes from a gas into a liquid

Ⓒ changes from a solid into to a liquid

Ⓓ changes from a liquid into a solid

SC.4.P.8.2

⑯ The table shows some properties of water in different states.

Solid	Liquid	Gas
Feels cold	?	has no definite shape

Which property should be put into the second column?

Ⓕ feels dry

Ⓖ tastes sour

Ⓗ has strong odor

Ⓘ fits the shape of its container

SC.4.P.8.2

17 A pan balance is used to measure a physical property of objects. The illustration below shows the measurement of the property of an apple.

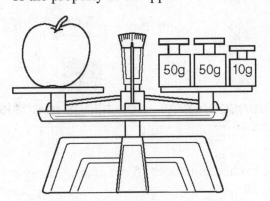

What property does the pan balance measure?

Ⓐ length

Ⓑ mass

Ⓒ shape

Ⓓ volume

SC.4.P.8.1

18 An artist is creating a special piece of art using fabric. It will be placed inside a box. To experience the art, visitors will place their hands into holes in the box and touch the art without being able to see it. What would be the **most** important characteristic to consider when choosing the fabric for the art piece?

Ⓕ odor

Ⓖ length

Ⓗ mass

Ⓘ texture

SC.4.N.1.1

19 Riley makes three balls out of modeling clay. He puts all of the clay balls on a balance and measures the total mass as 56 g. He then pushes the clay into one big ball and measures its mass. Which of the following would be a reasonable mass for the entire ball?

Ⓐ 53 g

Ⓑ 55 g

Ⓒ 56 g

Ⓓ 59 g

SC.4.P.8.3

20 Chang uses a balance to measure the mass of a toy truck. He records the mass in the table below. He then takes the truck apart and places all the parts on the balance.

	Mass
Whole truck	92 grams
Truck taken apart	?

What will Chang **most likely** record on his chart as the mass of the truck's parts?

Ⓕ 86 g

Ⓖ 88 g

Ⓗ 92 g

Ⓘ 98 g

SC.4.P.8.3

Name _____ Date _____

Magnetic Poles

Materials

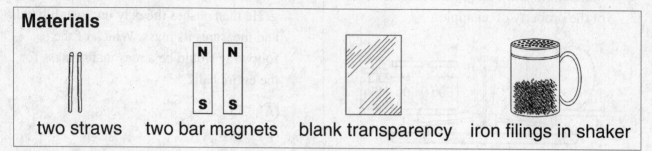

two straws   two bar magnets   blank transparency   iron filings in shaker

Procedure

1 Place the two straws on a flat table, parallel to each other and about 15 cm apart.

2 Place a bar magnet halfway between the straws, as shown in Figure A.

3 Place a blank transparency over the magnet and straws. Lightly sprinkle iron filings on top of the transparency, all over the magnet. Make a labeled sketch of the magnet and the pattern formed by the iron filings.

4 Use the transparency to pour the filings back into the shaker.

5 Repeat Steps 1, 2, and 3, but place the two magnets as shown in Figure B. Then repeat these steps again, placing the two magnets as shown in Figure C.

6 Write a paragraph to describe and explain your observations.

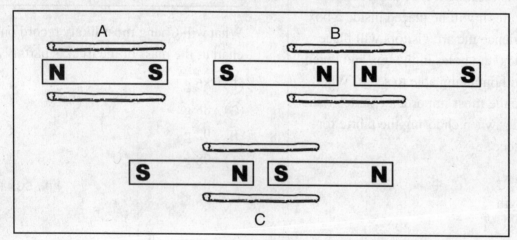

Teacher's Directions

Magnetic Poles

Materials Performance Task sheet, two straws, two bar magnets, blank transparency, iron filings in shaker

Time 30 minutes

Suggested Grouping groups of two to four students

Inquiry Skills observe, draw conclusions

Preparation Hints Pour iron filings into grated-cheese shakers or salt shakers with large holes. Make sure straws are about the same thickness as magnets.

Introduce the Task Ask students to describe a magnet. Guide them to use the term *poles* to describe the ends of a bar magnet. Tell them they are going to do an investigation to see the effect that poles have on iron filings and on each other. Model the setups they are to use.

Promote Discussion Ask students to describe the results of their investigation. Direct the discussion toward the fact that there was a "field" around each pole. Continue the discussion so that students comprehend that unlike poles attract each other and like poles repel each other. Ask students to display their drawings.

Scoring Rubric

Performance Indicators

_____ Works cooperatively with other team members.

_____ Follows written and oral directions.

_____ Makes three labeled drawings to show the positions of the magnets and iron filings.

_____ Writes a paragraph and concludes that like poles of a magnet repel and unlike poles attract.

Observations and Rubric Score

3   2   1   0

What Are Physical and Chemical Changes?

1 A physical change is a change that does not cause a new substance to form. Which is an example of a physical change?

(A) a glass breaking

(B) a dead plant rotting

(C) a candle wick burning

(D) an iron crowbar rusting

2 A change in color or smell is a sign of what?

(F) size change

(G) state change

(H) texture change

(I) chemical change

3 Chemical changes occur when the molecules of one substance are rearranged to form a different substance. Which of the following is a chemical change?

(A) bending

(B) burning

(C) freezing

(D) shredding

4 Daniel has a list of chores to do around the house. Which of his chores is an example of a chemical change?

(F) cooking eggs for breakfast

(G) oiling a squeaky door hinge

(H) sewing a hem on a pair of pants

(I) digging weeds in the flowerbeds

5 Chefs use physical and chemical changes in their kitchens. Which statement tells how a cook uses physical changes when making food?

(A) frying an egg

(B) rolling out pie crust

(C) baking biscuit dough in an oven

(D) waiting for a banana to ripen

How Can You Tell When a New Substance Forms?

1 A chemical change forms a new kind of matter. Which is a chemical change?

- (A) rusting steel
- (B) cutting bread
- (C) pouring water
- (D) breaking glass

2 When steel wool is soaked in water and then exposed to air, it slowly rusts. What do you observe when steel wool has rusted?

- (F) The steel wool turns red and brittle.
- (G) The steel wool turns white and soft.
- (H) The steel wool turns black and green.
- (I) The steel wool turns strong and shiny.

3 A plant or animal that has died will decay over time. Decaying is a chemical change. What observations show that decaying is a chemical change?

- (A) a change in size and shape
- (B) a change in color and smell
- (C) having the same temperature
- (D) having the same state of matter

4 Bonnie uses steel wool to sand model race-cars. She knows that steel wool can rust. Where should she store the steel wool to keep it from rusting?

- (F) in a dry place
- (G) in a wet place
- (H) in a dark place
- (I) in a damp place

5 When steel wool is exposed to water and air, it slowly rusts. Rusting is a chemical change. If you compare a piece of steel wool before it rusts with the same piece of steel wool after it rusts, what would you observe?

- (A) The steel wool is shiny and strong and stays shiny and strong.
- (B) The steel wool is shiny and strong and then becomes red and brittle.
- (C) The steel wool is a solid at first and then starts to melt into liquid metal.
- (D) The steel wool is a solid at first and then becomes part of the water mixture.

Matter and Its Changes

1 Salim blows up a new balloon and then lets the air out. He examines the physical change he caused to the balloon.

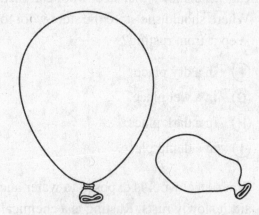

Which **best** describes the physical change in the balloon?

Ⓐ change in size

Ⓑ change in color

Ⓒ change in position

Ⓓ change in number of pieces

SC.4.P.9.1

2 Elise helps her teacher create a bulletin board showing different types of physical changes. The bulletin board has a folded piece of paper, a beach ball filled partially with air, and a piece of cloth with a rip in it. Which of the following could Elise add to the bulletin board to show another **type** of physical change?

Ⓕ a flat bicycle tire

Ⓖ a picture of melting ice

Ⓗ a piece of foil with a cut in it

Ⓘ a wire that has been bent

SC.4.P.9.1

3 Ella has to write a research paper on physical changes. Which gives the **best** definition of a physical change?

Ⓐ a change that gives off heat

Ⓑ a change that causes bubbles to form

Ⓒ a change in size, shape, or state

Ⓓ a change that makes a new substance

SC.4.P.9.1

4 Jayden adds salt to a pot of boiling water. Which **best** explains why adding salt causes a physical change?

Ⓕ the water changes color

Ⓖ the salt dissolves in the water

Ⓗ the water changes temperature

Ⓘ the salt burns in the boiling water

SC.4.P.9.1

5 Adela sees her grandmother's teapot on a shelf. The teapot is silver and has some tarnish on the outside. What does the tarnish indicate?

Ⓐ change of state

Ⓑ physical change

Ⓒ chemical change

Ⓓ change of texture

SC.4.P.9.1

6 Tony places some iron nails on a wet shelf in his garage. What will likely happen when the nails come in contact with air?

Ⓕ The nails will rust.

Ⓖ The nails will melt.

Ⓗ The nails will bend.

Ⓘ The nails will burn.

SC.4.P.9.1

7 Fireworks manufacturers create different colored explosions using different chemicals. A firework with copper can give off blue sparks. A firework with aluminum inside burns white. What do copper fireworks and aluminum fireworks have in common?

(A) Both decay at a slow rate.

(B) Both rust in contact with air.

(C) Both tarnish when they explode.

(D) Both explode because of a chemical reaction.

SC.4.P.9.1

8 A landscape designer suggests the Ling family place an iron railing on the patio that overlooks a lake. Mr. Ling thinks that the water from the lake, the iron railing, and the air will cause a problem over time. What might happen to the iron railing because of the water and air?

(F) The iron railing will rust.

(G) The iron railing will burn.

(H) The iron railing will bend.

(I) The iron railing will tarnish.

SC.4.P.9.1

9 Scuba divers use light sticks to light their way under water. To use a light stick, a scuba diver snaps the stick to mix two substances. The substances inside give off light when they mix. What information tells you that light sticks use a chemical reaction?

(A) Scuba divers use light sticks.

(B) The light stick can light up only once.

(C) Two substances mix when the light stick is snapped.

(D) The light sticks are the same as children's glow sticks.

SC.4.P.9.1

10 Bela is picking tomatoes from her garden. She finds a tomato on the ground that is soft and runny. Which sentence **best** describes what happened to the tomato?

(F) The tomato rotted, which is a chemical change.

(G) The tomato moved, which is a chemical change.

(H) The tomato deflated like a flat tire, which is a physical change.

(I) The tomato ignited like a firecracker, which is a chemical change.

SC.4.P.9.1

11 Sara is watching television when the power goes out. When she walks to the kitchen to get a candle, she knocks over a chair. She lights a match and holds it to the wick of the candle. She uses the light from the candle to find her way to the chair, which she picks up and sits in. Which of the events was a chemical change?

(A) losing power

(B) lighting the match

(C) knocking over the chair

(D) sitting in the chair

SC.4.P.9.1

12 While Lee is babysitting Jimmy, Jimmy falls and cuts his hand. Lee pours peroxide on the cut. The peroxide bubbles when it touches the blood. Finally, Lee puts a bandage on the cut. Which is an example of a chemical change?

(F) the hand bleeding

(G) the peroxide bubbling

(H) the bandage covering the cut

(I) Lee babysitting Jimmy

SC.4.P.9.1

13 Keeping a swimming pool safe to swim in takes a great deal of work. Which demonstrates how a chemical change keeps the water safe to swim in?

(A) running the water through a filter

(B) removing leaves from the water

(C) adding chlorine to kill bacteria

(D) vacuuming dirt from the pool

SC.4.P.9.1

14 Hardware stores help people make, build, and repair things around the house. Which describes something that could **most likely** cause a chemical change?

(F) sandpaper used to make wood smooth

(G) a drill that makes a hole in concrete or brick

(H) a grinder that turns a piece of metal into a key

(I) a powerful glue that is formed when two different liquids are mixed together

SC.4.P.9.1

15 Artists use chemical and physical changes when creating different works of art. Which statement **best** describes a physical change an artist might use?

(A) Saltwater gives a copper sculpture a green tarnish.

(B) Film and paper in a special liquid form a photograph.

(C) Soft gray clay is heated and becomes hard and white.

(D) Carving a piece of wood with a blade makes the wood into a bowl.

SC.4.P.9.1

16 Aliya's bike is made of steel. When she isn't riding her bike, she parks it outside on the back porch. One day it rained and Aliya's bike got wet. How can Aliya help keep her bike from rusting?

(F) wash her bike

(G) ride in the rain

(H) wipe the water off her bike

(I) spray her bike with the hose

SC.4.P.9.1

17 One spring, two families bought new metal furniture for their porches. Two years later, the Flaherty family's furniture is very rusty. Next door, the Ortiz family's furniture is not rusty at all.

Flaherty's Porch

Ortiz's Porch

Why is Flaherty's furniture rusty when the Ortiz family's furniture is not?

(A) The Ortiz's porch has a roof, so their furniture stays cool.

(B) The Ortiz's porch has a roof, so their furniture gets little wind.

(C) The Flaherty's porch has no roof, so their furniture stays in the sunlight.

(D) The Flaherty's porch has no roof, so their furniture gets wet when it rains.

SC.4.P.9.1, SC.4.N.1.3

18 Two friends used steel wool to sand model airplanes. When they finished, one girl put her steel wool on the dry workbench in the garage. The other girl rinsed her steel wool in water and set it on the dry workbench.

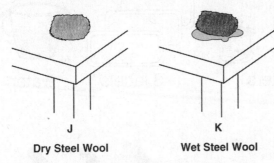

J
Dry Steel Wool

K
Wet Steel Wool

Which of the following would you expect to observe after a week has passed?

(F) Both pieces of steel wool have rusted.

(G) Steel wool J is the only piece of steel wool that has rusted.

(H) Steel wool K is the only piece of steel wool that has rusted.

(I) Neither piece of steel wool rusted.

SC.4.P.9.1, SC.4.N.1.3

19 A scientist was testing different materials to see which rusted the quickest. Each material was placed in water for the same amount of time and then stored in the same room. The scientist is trying to decide how often to observe the materials to see which ones rust the quickest. Which of the following should the scientist do?

(A) observe the materials once a month

(B) observe the materials once a week

(C) observe the materials once a day

(D) observe the materials every hour

SC.4.P.9.1, SC.4.N.1.3, SC.4.N.1.7

20 The class discussed different things they could do to a piece of wood. Which of the following would be a chemical change?

(F) The piece of wood could be ground up and made into mulch for a garden.

(G) The piece of wood could be broken up into smaller pieces to make tent pegs.

(H) The piece of wood could be nailed to another piece of wood.

(I) The piece of wood could be burned in a stove to heat some rooms.

SC.4.P.9.1

A Chemical Reaction?

Materials

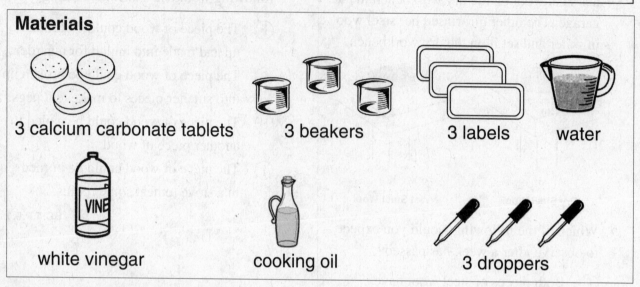

3 calcium carbonate tablets   3 beakers   3 labels   water

white vinegar   cooking oil   3 droppers

Procedure

1 Label one beaker *water*, the second beaker *white vinegar*, and the third beaker *cooking oil*.

2 Place a calcium carbonate tablet in each beaker.

3 To the first beaker, add water drop by drop until the tablet is covered. Record your observations in the data table below.

4 Repeat Step 3 with the second beaker, using white vinegar.

5 Repeat Step 3 with the third beaker, using cooking oil.

6 In the data table, indicate whether a chemical reaction took place in beakers 1, 2, and 3.

Beaker #	Liquid	Observations	Chemical Reaction?
#1			
#2			
#3			

A Chemical Reaction?

Materials Performance Task sheet, 3 calcium carbonate (antacid) tablets, 3 beakers, 3 labels, water, white vinegar, cooking oil, 3 droppers

Time 30 minutes

Suggested Grouping pairs

Inquiry Skills observe, record, analyze and interpret

Preparation Hints Provide safety goggles for each student. You can prepare the beakers in advance by labeling them and pouring the water, vinegar, and cooking oil into small paper cups for each group. About 10 mL (enough to cover the tablet) of each liquid per group should be adequate.

Introduce the Task Ask students what happens during physical changes and during chemical reactions. Tell students that they are going to observe whether two substances react. Remind them that one sign of a chemical reaction is production of a gas (bubbling). Their task is to determine in which case(s) a chemical reaction takes place.

Promote Discussion When students have finished, ask them to compare their observations with those of other pairs. Were the findings the same? Ask students which liquid caused a chemical reaction. (the vinegar) How could they tell? (A gas was released.) Which liquid caused a physical change? (Water; the tablet broke apart slightly.) Which liquid caused no change? (the oil)

Scoring Rubric

Performance Indicators
_____ Adds liquid to the three tablets and observes the results.
_____ Accurately records observations in the data table.
_____ Determines whether a chemical reaction has taken place in each case.
_____ Explains what the evidence was to indicate that a chemical reaction took place.

Observations and Rubric Score

     3   **2**   **1**   **0**

What Are Some Forms of Energy?

❶ Ellie plugs in a radio and turns it on. What change in energy takes place when she does this?

Ⓐ Light energy changes into sound energy.

Ⓑ Electrical energy changes into sound energy.

Ⓒ Sound energy changes into electrical energy.

Ⓓ Chemical energy changes into sound energy.

❷ Fossil fuels are the most common source of energy. What else is **true** of fossil fuels?

Ⓕ They are renewable.

Ⓖ They form quickly underground.

Ⓗ They can be made in a laboratory.

Ⓘ They are burned to release energy.

❸ A rolling ball has kinetic energy. What does it mean for an object to have kinetic energy?

Ⓐ The object is in motion.

Ⓑ The object has stored energy.

Ⓒ The object has used all of its energy.

Ⓓ The object is passing on its energy.

❹ Objects can have potential energy because of their position. Which object has potential energy?

Ⓕ book sitting on a table

Ⓖ hands turning on a clock

Ⓗ spinning wheels on a bike

Ⓘ flag flapping in the wind

❺ Objects may have potential energy or kinetic energy. How do potential energy and kinetic energy compare to each other?

Ⓐ Both describe objects at rest.

Ⓑ Both describe objects in motion.

Ⓒ Both are forms of mechanical energy.

Ⓓ An increase in one leads to an increase in the other.

Where Does Energy Come From?

1 Ada launches a ball into the air. It travels about 3 m. before it lands on the floor. What happens to the kinetic energy of the ball when it is on the floor?

Ⓐ The kinetic energy is lost.

Ⓑ The kinetic energy changes into heat.

Ⓒ The kinetic energy changes into potential energy.

Ⓓ The kinetic energy is the same after the ball stops.

2 Michael is using a spring on a dowel to send foam balls into the air. He keeps a supply of balls next to his equipment. If one of the balls falls off the table, what kind of energy change is taking place?

Ⓕ Potential energy is changing into kinetic energy.

Ⓖ Kinetic energy is changing into potential energy.

Ⓗ Kinetic energy is changing into electrical energy.

Ⓘ Potential energy is changing into magnetic energy.

3 Taylor tosses a ball into the air. Taylor knows that the energy of the ball changes as it leaves her hand, goes to its highest point in the air, and then comes back down. Which of the following **best** shows how the ball's energy changes?

Ⓐ kinetic energy → potential energy

Ⓑ potential energy → kinetic energy

Ⓒ kinetic energy → potential energy → kinetic energy

Ⓓ potential energy → kinetic energy → potential energy

4 Sarah is studying the energy of motion. She tapes a dowel onto a desk. Then she puts a 12-cm spring on the dowel. Next, she slips a foam ball onto the dowel. As she changes the length of the spring, she releases the ball into the air several times.

Length of spring (cm)	Distance traveled by ball (m)
10	2
8	2.5
6	4
4	6

What happens to the ball as Sarah changes the length of the spring?

Ⓕ When the spring is longer, the ball travels farther.

Ⓖ When the spring is longer, the ball does not travel.

Ⓗ When the spring is shorter, the ball travels farther.

Ⓘ When the spring is shorter, the ball does not travel.

5 Daniel's science class has to choose an example of potential energy changing into kinetic energy. Which could they pick?

Ⓐ sun warming a greenhouse

Ⓑ magnet attracting little pieces of iron

Ⓒ battery in a drawer

Ⓓ baseball as it leaves a pitcher's glove

What Is Sound?

1 Sarah has a thick rubber band and a thin rubber band. Sarah plucked each rubber band. If both bands are plucked in the same way, how would the pitch of the thicker one compare with the pitch of the thinner one?

(A) higher

(B) louder

(C) lower

(D) softer

2 Michael stretched a rubber band between his hands. Olivia pulled the rubber band and let it go. Then she wrote that they observed a sound. To hear a higher-pitched sound from the rubber band, what should Olivia do?

(F) Pull the rubber band harder.

(G) Stretch the rubber band less.

(H) Stretch the rubber band more.

(I) Pull the rubber band less.

3 Michelle plays a guitar. When she plays the highest string, she hears a sound. To hear a lower-pitched sound from that same highest string, what should she do?

(A) Tighten the string.

(B) Loosen the string.

(C) Play the string harder.

(D) Play the string more softly.

4 Students are making rubber bands vibrate. If one rubber band is thicker than another, what happens to the pitch?

(F) It is higher.

(G) It is lower.

(H) It is louder

(I) It is the same.

5 Imari is learning how to play a guitar. The pictures show her playing two notes.

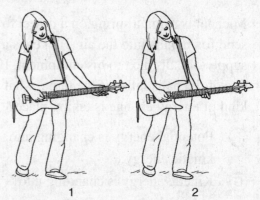

1   2

What happened to the sound from the string when she held it down the second time?

(A) It got lower.

(B) It got louder.

(C) It got softer.

(D) It got higher.

How Do People Use Energy from Wind and Water?

1 Many people around the world use fossil fuels to heat their homes and to provide electricity. The use of fossil fuels concerns environmental scientists because there is a limited supply of fossil fuels and burning them causes pollution. Which type of energy is considered a fossil fuel?

(A) hydroelectric

(B) oil

(C) solar

(D) wind

2 More and more people around the world are getting their electricity from renewable resources. Which word is another word for *renewable*?

(F) clean

(G) electric

(H) limited

(I) replaceable

3 One source of Earth's energy is fossil fuels. What is true about fossil fuels?

(A) They are unlimited.

(B) They are nonrenewable.

(C) They keep pollution out of the air.

(D) They take in energy when they are burned.

4 The energy of running water can be converted into other forms of usable energy. What do we call the kind of energy produced by running water?

(F) fossil fuels

(G) hydroelectric

(H) solar

(I) wind

5 One solar panel can generate enough energy for 5 homes. How many solar panels are needed to power a city that has 50,000 homes?

(A) 1,000 solar panels

(B) 5,000 solar panels

(C) 10,000 solar panels

(D) 50,000 solar panels

Energy and Its Uses

1 Eduardo cooks a pizza in a gas oven. Which form of energy cooks the pizza?

(A) chemical   (C) heat

(B) electrical   (D) light

SC.4.P.10.1

2 Akiko picks up a book from the ground. She drops it back on the ground. How does the book's energy before it is picked up compare to its energy after it falls?

(F) The book has the same potential energy before and after it falls.

(G) The book has more potential energy before it is picked up than it has after it falls.

(H) The book has more kinetic energy after it falls than it has before it is picked up.

(I) The book has less potential energy after it falls than it has before it is picked up.

SC.4.P.10.1

3 Sam pulls his sister in a wagon on a flat sidewalk. Which is the source of energy that moves the wagon?

(A) chemical energy in Sam's muscles

(B) kinetic energy from the rolling wheels

(C) potential energy from the ground below

(D) gravitational energy pulling on the wagon

SC.P.4.10.2

4 A book falls on the floor. Which is the **main** form of energy that results when the book strikes the floor?

(F) heat energy   (H) sound energy

(G) kinetic energy   (I) chemical energy

SC.P.4.10.1

5 Vanya toasts a piece of bread in a toaster connected to a wall outlet. Which is the source of energy for the toaster?

(A) heat energy   (C) electrical energy

(B) light energy   (D) chemical energy

SC.P.4.10.1

6 Solar energy is one type of alternative energy currently being investigated. Which of these is a benefit of solar energy?

(F) Solar energy is not renewable.

(G) Solar energy does not pollute the air.

(H) Solar energy is the most effective fossil fuel.

(I) Solar energy cannot be converted into other forms of energy.

SC.4.P.10.4

7 A town in Florida has enough solar panels to provide energy to each house in the town. One solar panel can generate enough energy for 4 homes. If the town has 8,000 solar panels, how many homes are in this Florida town?

(A) 2,000 homes   (C) 16,000 homes

(B) 4,000 homes   (D) 32,000 homes

SC.4.P.10.4

8 The pictures below show a boy and a girl playing musical instruments.

The boy's guitar makes a higher sound than the girl's drum. Which reason **best** describes why this might happen?

(F) The drum has a higher pitch than the guitar.

(G) The drum makes a louder sound than the guitar.

(H) The guitar's parts vibrate, but the drum's parts do not.

(I) The guitar's parts vibrate more quickly than the drum's parts.

SC.4.P.10.3

9 The picture below shows a rubber band stretched to two different lengths. The band can be pulled to the side and let go to make a sound.

Original length, 4 cm

A, stretched to 12 cm

B, stretched to 8 cm

What would you predict about the pitch of the sound of rubber band B compared to rubber band A?

(A) higher   (C) lower

(B) louder   (D) softer

SC.4.P.10.3, SC.4.N.1.4

10 The pictures below show the same rubber band stretched between thumbtacks on a board. Suppose you held the rubber band down with a pencil. When you plucked the band to the left of the pencil, the sound changed. Which has the highest pitch?

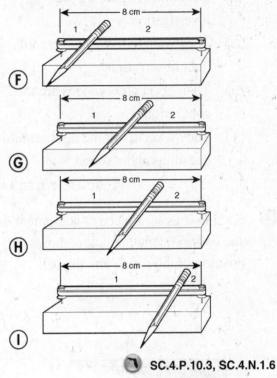

(F)

(G)

(H)

(I)

SC.4.P.10.3, SC.4.N.1.6

11 When you pluck a rubber band, it makes a sound. What can you do to make the sound softer?

(A) Stretch the band so it is longer.

(B) Loosen the band so it is shorter.

(C) Stop the band when it begins moving.

(D) Stretch the band less to the side before letting it go.

SC.4.P.10.3, SC.4.N.1.4

12 Matthew and Abigail are investigating the sound made by rubber bands. They listen to the sound. Then they carefully write what they heard. Which of the following gives the **best** reason that they do this?

(F) They want to plan a good investigation.

(G) They want to have good records of their observations.

(H) Their good observations are their conclusions.

(I) They want to ask the right scientific questions about sound.

SC.4.P.10.3, SC.4.N.1.6

13 Katrina is using a piece of equipment that she built. The picture below shows the position of the spring and the ball.

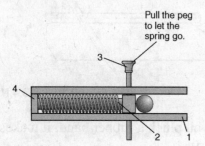

If Katrina squeezes the spring to half its length in the picture, what effect will that have on the ball?

(A) The ball will create more energy.

(B) The ball's kinetic energy will decrease.

(C) The ball's potential energy will increase.

(D) The ball's potential energy will decrease.

SC.4.P.10.1, SC.4.P.10.2, SC.4.N.1.1, SC.4.N.1.5

14 During an experiment, Corrine uses a piece of equipment to send a ball into the air. The picture below shows Corrine's equipment. It shows how the ball travels.

What kind of energy will the ball have just before it comes down?

(F) electrical   (H) magnetic

(G) kinetic   (I) potential

SC.4.P.10.1, SC.4.P.10.2

15 Tyler is studying the energy of motion. Tyler's equipment is shown below. Tyler decided to change the end of the spring from position 5 to position 4.

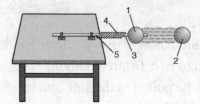

What happens to the ball when Tyler launches it?

(A) The ball does not move when the position changed.

(B) The ball goes farther than if the spring were still at position 5.

(C) The ball goes a shorter distance than if the spring were still at position 5.

(D) The ball goes the same distance as it would if the spring were still at position 5.

SC.4.P.10.2

16 Caleb and Imari are using a spring to send balls into the air. Caleb's ball travels 10 m. Imari squeezes the spring until it is shorter than Caleb's spring. How far is Imari's ball likely to go?

(F) 5 m   (H) 10 m

(G) 8 m   (I) 15 m

SC.4.P.10.1, SC.4.P.10.2, SC.4.N.1.1, SC.4.N.1.5

17 The following diagram illustrates the process of photosynthesis.

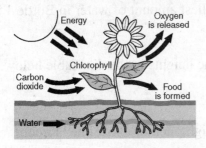

What type of energy is responsible for powering photosynthesis?

(A) light energy   (C) wind energy

(B) heat energy   (D) electrical energy

 SC.4.P.10.4

18 The image below shows a calculator.

What type of energy makes this calculator work?

(F) heat energy   (H) solar energy

(G) water energy   (I) wind energy

 SC.4.P.10.4

19 The circle graph below compares the amounts of energy from different sources used in the United States in 2007.

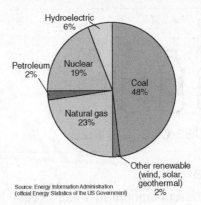

Source: Energy Information Administration (official Energy Statistics of the US Government)

How much more energy did nuclear power provide than hydroelectric power?

(A) 6%   (C) 17%

(B) 13%   (D) 19%

 SC.4.P.10.4

20 The energy of flowing water can be converted into other forms of energy. Which form of energy does flowing water possess that can be converted into other forms of energy?

(F) electrical energy

(G) gravitational energy

(H) kinetic energy

(I) wind energy

 SC.4.P.10.4

Compare Pitches

Materials

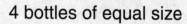

4 bottles of equal size

water

ruler

Procedure

1 Put a different amount of water in each bottle, from the smallest amount of water in Bottle 1 to the greatest amount of water in Bottle 4.

2 Measure the height of the water in each bottle, and record the heights in the data table below.

3 Predict how the different levels of water will affect pitch.

4 Blow across the mouth of Bottle 1. Does the sound have a high pitch or a low one? Record in the table your observation of the pitch.

5 Blow across the mouth of Bottle 2. Does the sound have a higher pitch or a lower pitch than the sound of Bottle 1? Blow again across the tops of Bottles 1 and 2 to make sure. Record your observations.

6 Repeat Step 5 with Bottle 3 and Bottle 4. Record your observations. Compare your prediction with the results you obtained.

	Bottle 1	Bottle 2	Bottle 3	Bottle 4
Height of water column				
Pitch of sound				

Compare Pitches

Materials Performance Task sheet, 4 bottles, water, ruler

Time 30 minutes

Suggested Grouping pairs or groups of three

Inquiry Skills observe, compare, infer

Preparation Hints Collect sets of four same-size bottles for students to use.

Introduce the Task Ask students to recall what they know about how trombones and other wind instruments change pitch. Make sure they understand that pitch is affected by the length of the air column and the change in frequency of the sound waves. Ask students to predict how different levels of water in a bottle will affect pitch.

Promote Discussion When students finish, ask them to share their results. Were their results similar? Did they find that the higher the water level, the higher the pitch? Ask students to explain the relationship between water level, the corresponding height of the column of air above the water, and pitch. (The higher the water level, the shorter the column of air. The shorter the column of air, the higher the pitch. This is because the shorter column of air in a fuller bottle vibrates at a higher frequency than the longer column of air in a less-full bottle.) Ask students to compare their predictions with their results.

Scoring Rubric

Performance Indicators
_____ Sets up and properly conducts experiment.
_____ Records data accurately for each bottle.
_____ Compares predictions with experimental results.
_____ Determines that the shorter the column of air, the higher the pitch.

Observations and Rubric Score
3   2   1   0

What Is Heat?

1 Blayne uses a thermometer to take a single reading of the water in a beaker. What is Blayne measuring?

  Ⓐ conduction rate

  Ⓑ temperature of the water

  Ⓒ amount of energy transferred from the beaker to the water

  Ⓓ amount of energy transferred from the water to the beaker

2 On a warm sunny day, a lizard sits on a rock. Which word explains why the lizard feels heat from the sun?

  Ⓕ convection

  Ⓖ friction

  Ⓗ gravity

  Ⓘ radiation

3 Jessie knows that conduction is the transfer of heat energy. Which transfer of heat energy is made through conduction?

  Ⓐ hand heats a snowball

  Ⓑ radiator warms a home

  Ⓒ boiling water heats pasta

  Ⓓ sun warms a greenhouse

4 Each picture shows a source of heat. Which picture shows heat transfer through convection?

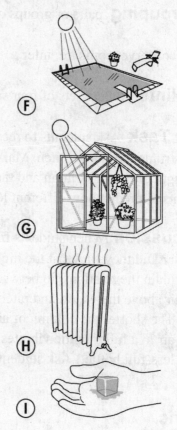

5 This table shows some sources of heat.

1	rays of the sun
2	electric space heater
3	oven with a fan
4	hot plate

Which source(s) will transfer heat through convection?

  Ⓐ 1 only

  Ⓑ 1 and 2 only

  Ⓒ 2 and 3 only

  Ⓓ 3 and 4 only

How Is Heat Produced?

1 Marie had a glass of water. The temperature of the water was 40 °C. Then Marie added some ice cubes to the water. After 10 min, what would the temperature of the water **most** likely be?

Ⓐ 50 °C

Ⓑ 45 °C

Ⓒ 40 °C

Ⓓ 35 °C

2 This thermometer was in the shade.

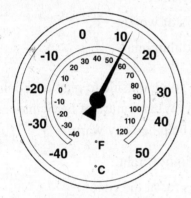

The sun began to shine on the thermometer. After 15 min, what would the temperature **most** likely be?

Ⓕ 25 °C

Ⓖ 25 °F

Ⓗ 10 °C

Ⓘ 10 °F

3 The sun is a heat source. Reptiles use the sun to control their body temperatures. Which statement describes how the sun affects the body temperature of a lizard?

Ⓐ When the lizard lies out in the sun, its body temperature increases.

Ⓑ When the lizard lies out in the sun, its body temperature decreases.

Ⓒ When the lizard lies out in the shade, its body temperature increases.

Ⓓ When the lizard lies out in the sun, its body temperature does not change.

4 Sometimes a region in Florida will have a heat wave. What happens to the temperature when the heat wave ends?

Ⓕ Temperatures rise.

Ⓖ Temperatures drop.

Ⓗ Temperatures stay the same.

Ⓘ Temperatures drop and then rise again.

5 Heat must flow to cause a material to change its temperature. All of these actions will change the temperature of an ice cube. Which action will change the ice cube's temperature the **most** in the shortest amount of time?

Ⓐ Place the ice cube in a freezer.

Ⓑ Place the ice cube on a countertop.

Ⓒ Place the ice cube in a glass of warm water.

Ⓓ Place the ice cube in a pot on the stove over a high flame.

What Are Conductors and Insulators?

① Philip is going to stir some soup he is cooking in a pot. The soup is very hot. He wants to use a spoon that will keep his hand from getting too hot. Which material would be **best** for the spoon?

Ⓐ aluminum

Ⓑ copper

Ⓒ steel

Ⓓ wood

② Nadia is planning to take a hot sandwich to school for lunch. She wants to wrap it in something to keep it warm. Which material would **best** keep the sandwich warm?

Ⓕ foam wrap

Ⓖ plastic wrap

Ⓗ waxed paper

Ⓘ aluminum foil

③ Asim is making a poster about conductors and insulators. Which of these objects should he list as a conductor?

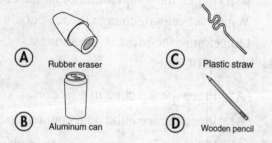

Ⓐ Rubber eraser　　Ⓒ Plastic straw

Ⓑ Aluminum can　　Ⓓ Wooden pencil

④ Bill is watching some builders while they are putting up the walls of a house. He notices that there is a small space between the outer and inner walls of the house. The builders then fill the space with a material. What did the builders **most** likely put into the space to prevent heat flow through the walls?

Ⓕ solid brick

Ⓖ fluffy fiber

Ⓗ layers of wood

Ⓘ thick aluminum

⑤ Keesha is going outside to play on a cold winter day. What feature of her winter coat will **most** help her stay warm?

Ⓐ It is lightweight.

Ⓑ It has fur at the edges.

Ⓒ It is thick and very fluffy.

Ⓓ It has a single layer of cloth.

Which Materials Are Conductors?

1 Akim fills a thermos with hot soup. How are the properties of the thermos important to heat transfer?

(A) The thermos provides heat to the soup.

(B) The thermos allows heat to pass through easily.

(C) The thermos blocks colder air from getting inside.

(D) The thermos does not allow heat to pass through easily.

2 Carmen wears wool socks with her winter boots to keep her feet warm. How is the wool important to heat transfer?

(F) Wool is an insulator that keeps Carmen's feet from losing heat.

(G) Wool is an insulator that provides heat to keep Carmen's feet warm.

(H) Wool is a conductor that transfers heat from Carmen's feet to her boots.

(I) Wool is a conductor that transfers heat from the socks to Carmen's skin.

3 Renata places a pat of butter on one end of a metal spoon. She heats the other end of the spoon. The butter melts. What is **not** true of Renata's experiment?

(A) Heat is conducted from a cooler object to a warmer object.

(B) Heat is conducted because the spoon and the butter are touching.

(C) Heat transfer will stop when the temperature of both materials is the same.

(D) The spoon and the butter are at different temperatures when the experiment starts.

4 An insulator is often used to help control an object's temperature. What is also **true** of an insulator?

(F) It slows energy transfer.

(G) It can also be a good conductor.

(H) It allows heat to pass through easily.

(I) It provides heat to keep materials warm.

5 Metal is a good conductor. Which object would be **most** useful if it were made of metal?

(A) thermos

(B) oven mitt

(C) muffin pan

(D) place mat

Heat

1 Carol orders some hot chocolate at a fast food restaurant. The cup is very hot. Which material would be best to wrap around the cup to prevent her hand from getting too hot?

(A) foam

(B) paper

(C) plastic wrap

(D) aluminum foil

SC.4.P.11.2

2 Amrit and his friends are building a playhouse in his backyard. Which material would best keep heat in during winter and keep heat out during summer?

(F) aluminum

(G) copper

(H) steel

(I) wood

SC.4.P.11.2

3 Oki's house gets very cold on winter nights. She has one thin blanket on her bed. What could she do to stay warmer at night?

(A) Add another thin blanket.

(B) Use two fluffy blankets instead.

(C) Add a fluffy blanket onto the thin blanket.

(D) Use a fluffy blanket instead of the thin blanket.

SC.4.P.11.2

4 Pat pours equal amounts of hot water into four cups. Each cup is made of a different material. She covers each cup and puts a thermometer into each.

Foam   Metal   Paper   Plastic

Which cup of water will **most** likely have the slowest temperature change?

(F) foam

(G) metal

(H) paper

(I) plastic

SC.4.P.11.2

5 The lunchbox that Jordan takes to school has soft, thick sides, as shown in the picture below.

Which material in the sides of the lunchbox **best** keeps the food warm that Jordan takes to school?

(A) air

(B) foil

(C) paper

(D) plastic

SC.4.P.11.2

6 Carl and his family went on a picnic. It was a hot day, and the sun was shining on the table where they put their things. Carl put a book on the table and covered it before going off to play. After an hour, he came back and was surprised to find that the book was not warm. Which material **most** likely covered the book?

(F) foam

(H) paper

(G) metal

(I) plastic

 SC.4.P.11.2

7 Lisa stirs some hot, apple cider with a metal spoon.

Which sentence explains what happens to the spoon?

(A) Heat from the hot liquid will warm the spoon until the spoon is hotter than the liquid.

(B) Heat from the hot liquid will warm the spoon until they are both the same temperature.

(C) Heat from the hot liquid will warm the spoon, but the liquid will remain hotter than the spoon.

(D) Heat from the hot liquid will not have any effect on a metal spoon, so the spoon will remain cool.

SC.4.P.11.1

8 Ossi knows that convection is the transfer of heat energy. Which transfer of heat energy is made through convection?

(F) A gas burner heats water.

(G) The sun warms a person.

(H) A hand warms an ice cube.

(I) An electric burner heats a pot.

SC.4.P.11.1

9 On a sunny day, Yolanda fills a small backyard pool with water. As time passes, the water warms. Which statement explains this effect?

(A) The sun heats the water through gravity.

(B) The sun heats the water through radiation.

(C) The sun heats the water through convection.

(D) The sun heats the water through conduction.

SC.4.P.11.1

10 Devon writes a summary of a lesson about heat. Which statement should Devon include in her summary?

(F) Heat always moves from cold objects to warm objects.

(G) Heat is transferred only by the radiant energy of the sun.

(H) Heat is a measure of the hotness or coldness of an object.

(I) Heat is the transfer of energy between objects of different temperatures.

SC.4.P.11.1

11 The pictures below show some sources of heat. Which example shows heat transfer through conduction?

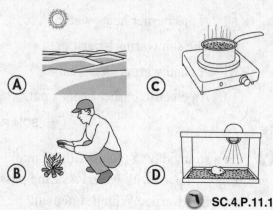

SC.4.P.11.1

12 The pictures below show some sources of heat. Which source transfers heat through radiation?

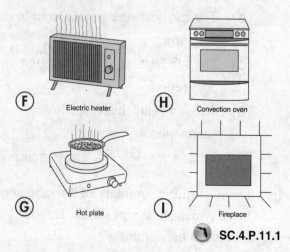

(F) Electric heater (H) Convection oven

(G) Hot plate (I) Fireplace

SC.4.P.11.1

13 As it gets warmer, the liquid inside a thermometer rises. Why does this happen?

(A) The liquid expands.

(B) The liquid changes color.

(C) The liquid changes into a solid.

(D) The liquid begins to evaporate.

SC.4.P.11.1

14 Emilio is building a model of a thermometer for his science fair project. Here is what he has built so far.

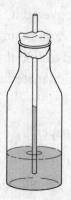

What should Emilio do to show that his model works like a real thermometer?

(F) Add more liquid to the bottle.

(G) Use a larger straw inside the bottle.

(H) Place numbers along the length of the straw.

(I) Put the thermometer in different temperatures.

SC.4.N.1.1, SC.4.N.3.1

15 Paula recorded the average temperatures for West Palm Beach, Florida, for four months during February through May. She wrote the average temperature for each month on a separate note card. However, she forgot to write the month on each card. Which is **most likely** the card for February?

(A) 72.4 °F   (C) 75.3 °F

(B) 81.7 °F   (D) 67.2 °F

SC.4.P.11.1

16 Venus is the hottest planet in our solar system. Its surface temperature averages around 480 °C (894 °F). Which is a reason that rivers are **not likely** to flow on Venus?

(F) Water cannot remain a liquid at this average temperature.

(G) Water would turn into solid ice at this average temperature.

(H) Water would lose all its heat to the surrounding atmosphere.

(I) Water would be found only in ponds and other small bodies of water.

SC.4.P.11.1, SC.4.N.1.1

17 Dan fills a bowl with hot water. He places four different objects in the bowl. Then he smears a bit of butter on each object, just above the water's surface. The picture below shows Dan's experiment.

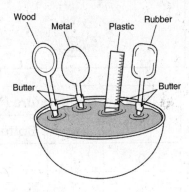

On which object will Dan **first** see butter melting?

(A) plastic ruler

(B) wood spoon

(C) metal spoon

(D) rubber spatula

SC.4.P.11.2

18 As Sammy walks barefoot on the sand, his feet feel very hot. What is the reason for this?

(F) The sand is transferring heat to his feet.

(G) Heat is passing from his feet to the sand.

(H) His feet and the sand are the same temperature.

(I) His feet have a higher temperature than the sand.

SC.4.P.11.1

19 The picture below shows a person lifting a pot off a stove.

At which point is heat transfer reduced?

(A) point A   (C) point C

(B) point B   (D) point D

SC.4.P.11.2

20 Marco handles four objects, which are shown below. Which object is **least** likely to change the way Marco's hand will feel if he holds the object?

SC.4.P.11.1

Observing Convection

Materials

tape

water

container

dyed ice cube

2 thermometers

clock

Procedure

❶ Set up the materials as shown. Fill the container with water. Tape one thermometer so that its bulb is near the top of the water.

❷ Wait 1 minute. Then record the temperatures in the table row for 0 min.

❸ Place the dyed ice cube in the water. Keep it away from the thermometers. DO NOT STIR THE WATER.

❹ Start timing. Record the temperatures every minute for 5 minutes. Observe the dye while you wait.

❺ Find the difference between the first and last temperatures for each thermometer. Record the differences in the table.

❻ Describe the convection that took place in the container. Use your data and observations.

❼ Predict what will happen to the temperature if you let the container sit for 10 more minutes.

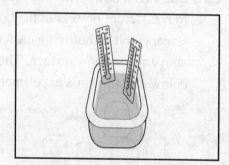

Time (min)	Temperature (°C)	
	Top	Bottom
0		
1		
2		
3		
4		
5		
Difference		

Observing Convection

Materials Performance Task sheet, 2 thermometers, clear tape, clock, 3-cup rectangular food-storage container, water, plastic jugs, ice-cube trays, dark food coloring

Time 30 minutes

Suggested Grouping pairs

Inquiry Skills observe, measure, record, predict

Preparation Hints Use containers of the size and shape listed. You will need access to a freezer. *Day before*: Fill ice-cube trays with water, and add 1 to 2 drops of dark food coloring to each well. Let the water freeze overnight. Fill the jugs with water, and let them sit overnight to reach room temperature. Tell students to tape the thermometers so that the bulb of one is at the bottom of the container and the bulb of the other is near the top, but covered with water.

Introduce the Task Review how convection starts in a pot on a stove: water at the bottom is heated, and then cool water moves in, pushing the heated water up. Tell students that the cool water is then heated and is also pushed up. In this investigation, they are going to observe convection by using two kinds of tools: a dye that makes cold water visible and two thermometers.

Promote Discussion Ask students to describe the path the cold water took as the ice cube melted. **What must have happened to the warmer water as the colder water moved in? How does the temperature data show the movement of the water?**

Scoring Rubric

Performance Indicators
_____ Follows the diagram to correctly set up the equipment.
_____ Makes all temperature readings and records them in the table.
_____ Describes the convection in detail.
_____ Bases prediction on own data and observations.

Observations and Rubric Score
3   2   1   0

Name _____ Date _____

What Is Motion?

1 To make sure your measurements are clear, it is important to use appropriate units. Which of these is a unit of distance?

(A) gram

(B) kilometer

(C) liter

(D) second

2 Cars, bicycles, and people can all be objects in motion. What is it about an object in motion that is constantly changing?

(F) acceleration

(G) position

(H) speed

(I) velocity

3 Friction can affect an object's motion. What is friction?

(A) a unit of the metric system

(B) a unit that is a measure of force

(C) energy in the form of pushing or pulling

(D) a force that opposes motion between two surfaces that are touching

4 Forces can affect the rate of an object's motion. Which of these is a force?

(F) acceleration

(G) gravity

(H) speed

(I) velocity

5 Jareem is riding his bike. He travels 30 km. It took him 3 hr. If Jareem was traveling at a constant speed, how fast was he traveling?

(A) 3 km/hr

(B) 10 km/hr

(C) 30 km/hr

(D) 90 km/hr

What Is Speed?

1 Karin's family lives in Melbourne. Her grandparents are coming to visit from Jacksonville. Karin knows that her grandparents left today at 10:00 a.m. Karin is looking at this map, and wants to know when she should expect her grandparents to arrive.

What does Karin need to know in order to figure this out?

Ⓐ the distance between the two cities

Ⓑ the average speed of her grandparents' car

Ⓒ how much luggage her grandparents are carrying

Ⓓ if there is construction between Melbourne and Clearwater

2 Mirsin Elementary School held a bike-a-thon. Below are some of the descriptions of the bike-a-thon. Which statement describes one aspect of velocity?

Ⓕ The bike-a-thon took place at Lake Ponci.

Ⓖ Many bikers began riding early in the morning.

Ⓗ More than 75 students rode in the bike-a-thon.

Ⓘ The bike path looped around the park from east to west.

3 Liu and Simone did an experiment about speed and velocity. Their data is in the following table.

Car	Distance traveled (m)	Time taken (sec)	Direction of motion
red	10	5	west
blue	20	20	east

What is the velocity of the red car?

Ⓐ 1 m/sec   Ⓒ 2 m/sec, west

Ⓑ 2 m/sec   Ⓓ 10 m/sec

4 Which statement describes a change in velocity?

Ⓕ Maria rode faster as she biked down the hill.

Ⓖ Maria rode her bike at a steady pace on a flat road.

Ⓗ Maria slowed down as she climbed a hill on her bike.

Ⓘ Maria slowed down to turn the corner and bike back home.

5 Mrs. Panetta's science class was studying motion. The data table shows the results of an experiment.

Student	Distance tennis ball rolled (m)	Time (sec)
Alicia	18	3
Jorge	21	7
Alex	15	3
Lucy	15	5

Which students had tennis balls that rolled at the same speed?

Ⓐ Alicia & Alex   Ⓒ Lucy & Jorge

Ⓑ Alex & Lucy   Ⓓ Alicia & Jorge

Forces and Motion

1 To make sure your measurements are clear, it is important to use appropriate units. Which of these is a unit of time?

(A) kilogram (C) milliliter

(B) meter (D) minute

SC.4.P.12.1

2 Velocity is a measurement related to motion. What is velocity?

(F) the rate at which acceleration changes

(G) a force that opposes motion between two surfaces that are touching

(H) a measure of both the speed and direction of a moving object

(I) a measure of how fast something moves; velocity is the same as speed

SC.4.P.12.2

3 To make sure your measurements are clear, it is important to use appropriate units. Which of these is a unit of speed?

(A) grams per liter (g/L)

(B) miles per hour (mph)

(C) liters per minute (L/min)

(D) hours per kilogram (hr/kg)

SC.4.P.12.2

4 Forces can affect the rate of an object's motion. Which of these is a force?

(F) acceleration (H) speed

(G) friction (I) velocity

SC.4.P.12.2

5 A train travels 200 km in the same direction in 2 hr. What is this train's velocity?

(A) 2 km/hr (C) 200 km/hr

(B) 100 km/hr (D) 400 km/hr

SC.4.P.12.2

6 Kinan ran for 1 mi at a speed of 8 min/mi. How long did it take Kinan to run 4 mi at the same rate?

(F) 2 min (H) 32 min

(G) 8 min (I) 64 min

SC.4.P.12.2

7 Ashwath walked for 3 hr at a speed of 10 km/hr. How far did Ashwath walk?

(A) 3 km (C) 30 km

(B) 10 km (D) 300 km

SC.4.P.12.2

8 Astronauts in outer space float because one of the forces we experience on Earth is very small in space. Which force is it?

(F) gravity (H) velocity

(G) friction (I) acceleration

SC.4.P.12.2

9 Whitney walks from her house to school, a distance of 1 mi. It takes her 14 min. How long will it take Whitney to walk home from school if, on her way, she walks at a rate of 1 mi/7 min?

(A) 7 min (C) 21 min

(B) 14 min (D) 28 min

SC.4.P.12.2

10 The following line graph shows an object's distance over time.

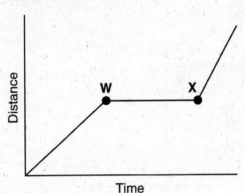

What is happening to the object between points W and X?

(F) It is not moving.

(G) It is speeding up.

(H) It is slowing down.

(I) It has acceleration.

 SC.4.P.12.2

11 Velocity and speed are both measurements describing an object's motion. What is a difference between velocity and speed?

(A) Speed depends on acceleration, but velocity does not.

(B) Speed does not depend on direction, but velocity does.

(C) Speed depends on velocity, but velocity does not depend on speed.

(D) Velocity only depends on friction, but speed only depends on gravity.

 SC.4.P.12.2

12 Three students are in a race. The students' starting points and the finish line are shown in the following diagram.

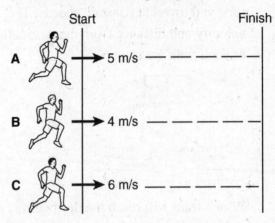

Which runner will win the race?

(F) Runner A will win the race.

(G) Runner B will win the race.

(H) Runner C will win the race.

(I) It will be a three-way tie.

 SC.4.P.12.2

13 The diagram below shows two heavy balls being held in position with four ropes.

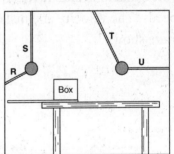

Which rope, if cut, will flip the box upward?

(A) rope R   (C) rope T

(B) rope S   (D) rope U

 SC.4.P.12.2

14 Three trains, all traveling from different directions, are heading toward the same destination. All three trains left at the same time and travel at constant speeds. The velocity and distance from the destination of each train are shown.

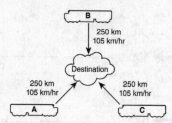

Which train will reach the destination first?

(F) Train A will be first.

(G) Train B will be first.

(H) Train C will be first.

(I) All three trains will reach the destination at the same time.

SC.4.P.12.2

15 Three people are traveling in their cars heading toward the supermarket. All three cars left at the same time and travel at constant speeds. The velocity and distance of each car are shown.

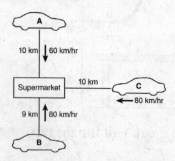

Which car will reach the supermarket first?

(A) Car A will be first.

(B) Car B will be first.

(C) Car C will be first.

(D) All the cars will reach the supermarket at the same time.

SC.4.P.12.2

16 Benny drops a ball off a bridge. The ball drops straight down, as shown in the diagram.

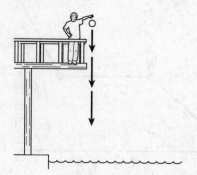

What happens to the ball as it falls?

(F) Its speed and acceleration stay the same.

(G) Both its speed and acceleration increase.

(H) Its speed decreases, but its acceleration increases.

(I) Its speed increases, but its acceleration decreases.

SC.4.P.12.2

17 The table shows the travel times and distances for four cars.

Car	Distance in kilometers (km) and miles (mi)	Time (hr)
A	300 km (about 185 mi)	3
B	200 km (about 125 mi)	2
C	400 km (about 250 mi)	4
D	300 km (about 185 mi)	2

Imagine that the speed limit was 110 km/hr, or 70 mph. Which car drove faster than the speed limit?

(A) A   (C) C

(B) B   (D) D

SC.4.P.12.2, SC.4.N.1.1

Name _____ Date _____

18 Mani traveled by car from Tallahassee to Pensacola.

Each of the following statements about Mani's car is true. Which statement describes the car's velocity?

(F) The car is traveling west at 80 km/hr.

(G) The car has stopped for gas at a service station.

(H) The car is traveling at the speed limit posted on the highway.

(I) The car is moving faster than any other car on the highway.

 SC.4.P.12.2

19 Skateboarding was first started in the 1950s, when all across California surfers got the idea of trying to surf on streets. Today, many people enjoy skateboarding. What change could a skateboarder make to increase the speed of a skateboard?

(A) Make a longer ramp so it is not as steep.

(B) Make a ramp as smooth and slick as possible.

(C) Begin skateboarding from the middle of a ramp.

(D) Wear a heavy backpack while skateboarding on a ramp.

 SC.4.P.12.2

20 Nick investigated velocity.

Object 1	13 meters	3 seconds
Object 2	9 meters	4 seconds
Object 3	22 meters	7 seconds

What is missing from his data table on velocity?

(F) the distance the object traveled

(G) the direction the object traveled

(H) time taken to travel the distance

(I) time taken to complete the experiment

 SC.4.N.1.5 | SC.4.P.12.2

Name _____ Date _____

Student Task

Bobsled Races

Materials

oil

petroleum jelly

water in spray bottle

heavy bolt

stack of books

tape measure or ruler

Procedure

Using the heavy bolt for a bobsled, compare three surfaces to find out which one allows the bolt to travel the farthest. Your teacher will provide each team with three tracks that are lined with aluminum foil.

1 Lightly cover each of the tracks with a different material (oil, petroleum jelly, or water).

2 Predict which surface will allow the bobsled to travel the farthest.

3 Test your prediction. Prop up the tracks, one at a time, on the stack of books. Give the same push to the bobsled on each track.

4 Record the distances in the data table. Was your prediction correct?

Track	Distance Traveled from Top of Ramp
Track with oil	
Track with petroleum jelly	
Track with water	

Bobsled Races

Materials Performance Task sheet, oil, petroleum jelly, water in spray bottle, heavy bolt, stack of books, tape measure or ruler, tracks made by the teacher in advance

Time 30 minutes

Suggested Grouping groups of three or four

Inquiry Skills predict, experiment, observe, record

Preparation Hints Make three tracks for each group of students. First, cut identical strips of poster board; the strips should be about 8 cm wide and 60–90 cm long. Cover each strip with aluminum foil, folding the foil around the edges. Fold up the long sides of each strip about 2 cm to keep the bobsled from falling off. Alternatively, you may wish to have students construct the bobsled tracks. Make sure there is enough space in the room for students to conduct their trials.

Introduce the Task Begin the activity by asking students what kinds of things help reduce friction (oil, smooth ice). Then have students name things that create more friction (bumpy ice, other rough surfaces). Tell students that they will conduct an investigation to see what kind of surface allows a small, heavy object—their bolt "bobsled"—to travel the farthest.

Promote Discussion When students finish, have the groups compare results. Are they the same or different? If different, can students explain why? Were their predictions correct?

Scoring Rubric

Performance Indicators

_____ Coats each track surface with one material: oil, petroleum jelly, or water.

_____ Measures distance accurately with a tape measure or ruler.

_____ Records data in the table.

_____ Compares results to prediction.

Observations and Rubric Score

3   2   1   0

How Do Plants Reproduce?

1 An empress tree is a flowering plant that grows in Florida. This tree's flowers have blue and violet markings. What is the **main** role of the colored markings on the flowers?

(A) to protect the plant from the sun

(B) to produce pollen for reproduction

(C) to attract insects to carry pollen

(D) to help disperse seeds to other parts of the local environment

2 The cedar tree is a nonflowering plant. The orange blossom tree is a flowering plant. Both trees have similar life cycles. What is the order of events in the life cycles of both plants?

(F) seed, pollination, seed dispersal, fertilization

(G) pollination, seed, seed dispersal, fertilization

(H) fertilization, pollination, seed, seed dispersal

(I) pollination, fertilization, seed, seed dispersal

3 The Florida maple tree is a flowering plant. The Florida longleaf pine tree is a nonflowering plant. Both trees go through various stages in their life cycles. Which stage is found in the life cycles of **both**?

(A) making cones

(B) making seeds

(C) making fruits

(D) making flowers

4 In the winter of 2006, millions of honeybees vanished from their hives throughout the country. No one was sure why the bees disappeared. However, everyone was concerned. Why were people concerned about what happened to the honeybees?

(F) Bees help with seed dispersal.

(G) Bees help protect seeds in nonflowering plants.

(H) Bees play a very important role as plant pollinators.

(I) Bees protect seeds until they start to germinate into seedlings.

5 The table lists some features of the possum grape vine.

Possum Grape Vine Plant	
Feature	**Description**
flower	yellow-green
growth pattern	tall-climbing
leaf	heart-shaped
stem	woody

The life cycle of a possum grape vine includes sexual reproduction. Which feature of the plant is used for sexual reproduction?

(A) flower

(B) growth pattern

(C) leaf

(D) stem

What Factors Affect Germination Rate?

1 Eli is studying germination in science class. The class is using bean seeds to explore what things seeds need to germinate. What is one thing Eli can do to test whether bean seeds need soil to germinate?

  (A) He can germinate a bean seed in soil and remove it to see if it grows.

  (B) He can plant a bean seed in poor soil and see how much longer it takes to germinate.

  (C) He can place a bean seed in a plastic bag with soil and water to see if it germinates.

  (D) He can place a bean seed in a plastic bag with a paper towel and water to see if it germinates.

2 Mr. Solomon's class is testing different conditions for germinating bean seeds. Which is the **best** way for them to study how the amount of water affects the rate of germination of the bean seeds?

  (F) Give the seeds large amounts of water and watch to see if any of them will germinate.

  (G) Give the seeds no water and wait to see if any of the seeds will germinate.

  (H) Give the seeds different amounts of water and record when each seed germinates.

  (I) Give each seed the same amount of water and watch to see which one germinates first.

3 Caspar plants four bean seeds. He waters the first seed twice a day, the second seed once a day, the third seed every other day, and the fourth seed not at all. Which seed can he expect to germinate first?

  (A) the seed he waters twice a day

  (B) the seed he waters once a day

  (C) the seed he waters every other day

  (D) the seed he does not water

4 Maria is experimenting with bean seeds to see if different fertilizers will make seeds grow taller than seeds grown without fertilizer. She plants several seeds in soil with different types of fertilizer. Which of the following does she need to have a controlled experiment?

  (F) bean seed that gets no fertilizer

  (G) seed other than a bean seed

  (H) bean seed that gets different amounts of the same fertilizer

  (I) bean seed that gets fertilizer added half way through the experiment

5 Jing planted two bean seeds in the same kind of soil. She gave them equal amounts of water and sunlight, but she kept the seeds at different temperatures. Each day she recorded whether or not the seeds had germinated. What was the variable?

  (A) amount of water

  (B) type of soil used

  (C) amount of sunlight

  (D) temperature of the seeds

How Do Animals Reproduce?

1 Elijah is preparing for a test on animal life cycles. He needs to remember how some animals go through metamorphosis. Which animal would be an example of an animal that goes through metamorphosis?

(A) coyote

(B) sea turtle

(C) grasshopper

(D) nurse shark

2 Benito finds a quail's nest while on a hike. He notices that a mother quail has eggs in the nest. What is likely to happen next in the life cycle of the quail eggs?

(F) flying

(G) growing

(H) hatching

(I) reproducing

3 Jihn walks on a sand dune and accidentally disturbs the burrow of a beach mouse and its pups. The pups are small and still nursing. What stage in the life cycle of the pups is this?

(A) birth

(B) growth

(C) maturity

(D) reproduction

4 Sasha notices an object on the ground near the nature trail.

Which type of animal could be the parent of this offspring?

(F) coyote

(G) raccoon

(H) robin

(I) skunk

5 Animals can be born and raised in many ways. Some animals lay eggs, others give birth to live young, and others are born and raised in pouches. Which animal gives birth to live young?

(A) ant

(B) chipmunk

(C) frog

(D) fish

What Are Heredity, Instincts, and Learned Behaviors?

1 Jake found that more than half the students in his class have brown eyes. How is eye color in humans classified?

Ⓐ behavior

Ⓑ characteristic

Ⓒ structure

Ⓓ trait

2 Animals in the wild learn to do many things. When do **most** animals learn their behaviors?

Ⓕ when they are born

Ⓖ when they are adult

Ⓗ when they are young

Ⓘ when they get a reward

3 One kind of moth lives on the bark of trees. In areas where the trees and moths are located near factories, their color is dark. Where there are no factories, the same kinds of moths and trees are light colored. What is the **most likely** cause for this change in color?

Ⓐ diet

Ⓑ instinct

Ⓒ environment

Ⓓ learned behavior

4 Canada geese travel north when the weather gets warm in the spring. Then they travel south when it gets cold in the late fall. Suppose that the spring temperature stayed cold two weeks longer than usual. How would that change the behavior of the geese?

Ⓕ They would not travel north at all.

Ⓖ They would travel north at the usual time.

Ⓗ They would travel north about two weeks later.

Ⓘ They would travel north about two weeks earlier.

5 Hurricanes in Florida damage trees. If a pine tree loses half of its branches, what will its offspring look like?

Ⓐ They will have no branches.

Ⓑ They will have twice as many branches.

Ⓒ They will have the normal number of branches.

Ⓓ They will have half the normal number of branches.

Life Cycles and Growth

1 The pictures below show behaviors of animals and people. Which is an inherited behavior?

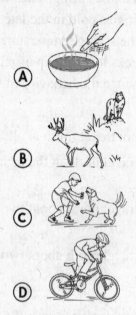

(A)

(B)

(C)

(D)

SC.4.L.16.3

2 An animal's environment can change some of its physical traits. Which trait can be changed by the environment?

(F) gills on a tadpole

(G) stripes on a zebra

(H) color of a pink flamingo

(I) type of hair on a dog's coat

SC.4.L.16.2

3 An arctic hare is brown in the summer and white in the winter. What is the **most** likely cause of this change?

(A) learned behavior

(B) instinctive behavior

(C) effect of environment

(D) beginning of hibernation

SC.4.L.16.2

4 The picture below shows a Florida panther stalking its prey.

Where does the panther learn this behavior?

(F) by itself

(G) from its mother

(H) from its instincts

(I) from other panther cubs

SC.4.L.16.3

5 Sameh looks a lot like other members of his family. Which is a trait that Sameh probably did **not** inherit from his parents?

(A) size of his feet

(B) shape of his ears

(C) color of his eyes

(D) length of his hair

SC.4.L.16.2

6 While researching opossums, Kilie came across the following picture.

What classification **best** describes the opossum?

(F) amphibian   (H) marsupial

(G) hatchling   (I) reptile

SC.4.L.16.4

7 The tussock moth caterpillar can cause many problems for people in Florida. The webs that the caterpillars spin are very sticky and are hard to remove. In what stage of its life cycle would the moth be when it is in a web?

(A) adult   (C) larva

(B) egg   (D) pupa

 SC.4.L.16.4

8 Florida is home to the great siren, a very large salamander. This animal is sometimes called a mud eel, but it is not an eel. Just like frogs, salamanders lay eggs that become tadpoles. At what stage of metamorphosis can a salamander lay eggs?

(F) adult   (H) larva

(G) egg   (I) pupa

SC.4.L.16.4

9 Some insects go through incomplete metamorphosis. Others go through complete metamorphosis. What stage is part of complete metamorphosis, but not incomplete metamorphosis?

(A) adult   (C) nymph

(B) egg   (D) pupa

SC.4.L.16.4

10 Animals that go through incomplete metamorphosis spend some time as nymphs. Which statement is **true** about nymphs?

(F) Nymphs are fully developed and can lay eggs.

(G) Nymphs look nothing like adults of the same animal.

(H) Nymphs molt as they grow from an immature animal to an adult.

(I) Nymphs spin cocoons so that they can rest and change form.

 SC.4.L.16.4

11 The coontie plant is the only cycad native to the United States. The cones of a coontie plant are very close to the ground.

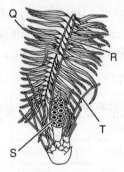

In which structure of the plant do the seeds develop?

(A) Q   (C) S

(B) R   (D) T

 SC.4.L.16.4

12 The life cycles of all seed plants involve certain steps. One of these steps is shown below.

Which step occurs **after** the step shown above?

Ⓕ death

Ⓖ germination

Ⓗ maturity

Ⓘ reproduction

SC.4.L.16.4

13 The Florida skullcap is a flowering plant. Scientists carefully monitor this plant. In one area alone, scientists observed this change in the number of Florida skullcaps.

Year	Florida skullcaps
2008	550
2009	2,000

What is a possible explanation for the increase in the number of Florida skullcaps?

Ⓐ a decrease in the rate of seed germination

Ⓑ an increase in the number of pollinators in the area

Ⓒ a decrease in the number of pollen grains released by an anther

Ⓓ an increase in the number of cones produced to protect the seeds

SC.4.L.16.1

14 Poison ivy grows in a wide range of habitats—from moist, shady areas to open, dry areas. The illustration shows a poison ivy plant.

Poison ivy produces pollen during its life cycle. How can you tell this by looking at the picture?

Ⓕ large leaf size

Ⓖ presence of cones

Ⓗ development of seeds

Ⓘ presence of a bee on the tiny flowers

SC.4.L.16.1

15 The southern red oak tree produces acorns. A single acorn can grow into a red oak that is 30 meters (about 100 feet) tall. What must an acorn contain?

Ⓐ a cone

Ⓑ a flower

Ⓒ a pollinator

Ⓓ a seed

SC.4.L.16.4

16 Many plants produce seeds that are dispersed by animals. What would **most likely** be found on seeds that are dispersed by sticking to the fur of an animal?

Ⓕ fan-like blades

Ⓖ hairs

Ⓗ hooks

Ⓘ wings

SC.4.L.16.1

Name _____ Date _____

Unit 9

17 A scientist is studying how quickly a seed germinates. She keeps the soil, amount of light, and water the same. She puts one seed in a room that is 5 °C, one in a room that is 10 °C, one in a room that is 15 °C, and the last seed in a room that is 20 °C. What variable is she testing?

(A) light   (C) temperature

(B) soil   (D) water

SC.4.L.16.1

18 A scientist is testing how different substances added to water affect the rate of germination of bean seeds. He plants several beans and waters them all with different solutions. Which of the following is the control in his experiment?

(F) seed watered with saltwater

(G) seed watered with plain water

(H) seed watered with sugar water

(I) seed watered with vinegar water

SC.4.L.16.1

19 Teleza planted two seeds in the same soil but in different pots, gave them the same amount of water and sunlight, but kept the soils at different temperatures.

2° C   15° C

What can Teleza conclude about how soil temperature affects the rate of germination of bean seeds?

(A) The seeds grow faster at 2 °C.

(B) The seeds grow slower at 15 °C.

(C) The seeds grow faster at 15 °C.

(D) The temperature of the soil does not affect the rate of germination.

SC.4.L.16.1

20 Joseph's bean plants were about the same size. They had the same amounts of soil and sunlight. They were kept in the same room. The chart shows the total amount of water Joseph gave each seed during the week and how much they grew. Now he wants to know what he did that made the plants grow different heights.

Plant	Water received for the week (mL)	Growth for the week (cm)
A	250	5
B	250	1
C	250	4

What information did Joseph forget to record that could help him?

(F) how tall the plants were when the week ended

(G) how much water each plant received each day

(H) how tall the plants were when the week started

(I) how tall the plants were at both the beginning and end of the week

SC.4.L.16.1

Unit Benchmark Test
© Houghton Mifflin Harcourt Publishing Company

AG 89

Grade 4 • Assessment Guide • Florida

Describe Important Events

Materials

colored pencils or markers

paper

Procedure

1 Draw a comic strip or a series of pictures that shows how your development has been influenced by heredity and by environment.

2 First, think about your life from infancy to the present. Choose five or six events that have taken place in your growth and development. Explain how each event was influenced by heredity and by environment.

3 Don't forget to label your drawings and to add dialogue or explanations as needed. Make sure to use the correct time order to tell what happened.

4 Choose one of the events to share with a partner or your teacher.

Describe Important Events

Materials Performance Task sheet, colored pencils or markers, paper

Time 25–30 minutes

Suggested Grouping individuals

Inquiry Skills order, draw conclusions, communicate

Preparation Hints If you plan to use large sheets of paper, you may have to rearrange the room to allow space for students to work.

Introduce the Task Remind students of some traits and behaviors that are influenced by heredity and of others that are influenced by environment. Explain to students that they will be examining their own life cycles and choosing five or six events in their growth and development that were influenced by heredity and environment. Allow students to be creative, if they wish.

Promote Discussion Do not ask students to share their comic strips with the class. Instead, hold a general discussion of the ways in which heredity and environment affect development.

Scoring Rubric

Performance Indicators
_____ Illustrates important life events.
_____ Understands how heredity and environment influenced each event.
_____ Draws conclusions about the influence of heredity and environment on growth and development.
_____ Communicates the importance of selected events to his or her development.

Observations and Rubric Score
3   2   1   0

How Do Organisms Change With the Seasons?

1 In a forest, there is little growth of plants during winter. What is the **main** reason this would affect deer in the forest?

(A) There would be less food.

(B) There would be less water.

(C) There would be less shade.

(D) There would be less shelter.

2 It is spring and Yi Min is going on a nature walk. Which of the following will Yi Min **most** likely see?

(F) budding plants

(G) dormant plants

(H) plants dropping fruit

(I) plants losing their leaves

3 Aaron is visiting a national park. The ranger tells Aaron that he is unlikely to see any ground squirrels because it is winter. Which of the following is the **most** likely reason Aaron would not see any ground squirrels?

(A) The ground squirrels migrated.

(B) The ground squirrels have died out.

(C) The ground squirrels are hibernating.

(D) The ground squirrels are gathering food.

4 During the spring, bears eat mainly grass. During the summer, bears also eat birds' eggs and fish. During the fall, bears eat ripe berries. Why do bears change their diet during the seasons?

(F) Each food offers different nutrients.

(G) Different food is available each season.

(H) Bears live in different areas each season.

(I) Bears like more food in the spring and summer.

5 In the fall, whooping cranes migrate from Wisconsin to Florida. What is the **main** reason the cranes leave Wisconsin for Florida?

(A) Wisconsin's ground freezes, and the birds cannot get any food.

(B) Wisconsin is too hot in the winter, and the birds prefer cool weather.

(C) Florida's level of sunlight provides better warmth than Wisconsin's sunlight.

(D) Florida has more rain in the winter, and Wisconsin only gets a small amount of rain.

How Do Organisms Obtain and Use Food?

1 Decomposers break down wastes and dead things for food. Some decomposers include mushrooms, bacteria, and earthworms. Which of these could provide food for a decomposer?

(A) large rocks

(B) fallen leaves

(C) small insects

(D) rays of sunlight

2 Mika follows a vegan diet. This means she does not eat meat or any other animal products. She gets all of the nutrients she needs from plant products. Which word describes Mika?

(F) consumer

(G) decomposer

(H) omnivore

(I) producer

3 Plants and animals are known as producers and consumers. This means that they make and use something. What is it that plants produce (make) and animals consume (use)?

(A) cells

(B) food

(C) sunlight

(D) water

4 The pictures below show different organisms, or living things. Which organism uses photosynthesis to get food?

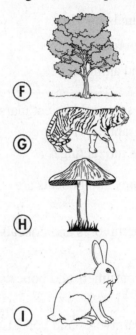

(F)

(G)

(H)

(I)

5 Hyenas, vultures, and opossums are scavengers. They get their food from eating dead things. Many people classify scavengers as decomposers. Others call them consumers. Why can scavengers be considered consumers?

(A) They eat producers.

(B) They eat consumers.

(C) They make energy from food.

(D) They get food from dead things.

What Are Food Chains?

1 Food chains have three kinds of consumers. Which describes an herbivore?

- (A) eats only plants
- (B) eats only animals
- (C) makes its own food
- (D) eats plants and animals

2 In the Everglades, some rabbits eat marsh grass. Bobcats eat rabbits. How are bobcats and rabbits interacting?

- (F) Rabbits are prey and bobcats are predators.
- (G) Rabbits are herbivores and bobcats are prey.
- (H) Rabbits are consumers and bobcats are producers.
- (I) Rabbits are carnivores and bobcats are herbivores.

3 In a forest, deer eat plants. Snakes eat small animals and birds. Raccoons eat mice, insects, fruits, and plants. What is the raccoon?

- (A) carnivore
- (B) herbivore
- (C) omnivore
- (D) producer

4 In a desert food chain, wild pigs called peccaries eat cactus. Then coyotes eat peccaries. In a forest food chain, deer eat plants. Then wolves eat deer. How does energy move in both of these food chains?

- (F) from producers to consumers
- (G) from consumers to producers
- (H) from scavengers to herbivores
- (I) from consumers to consumers

5 In a grassland food chain, grasshoppers eat grass and meerkats eat grasshoppers. What is the main role of the grasshopper in this food chain?

- (A) make a new habitat
- (B) be a source of energy
- (C) clear grass for space to live
- (D) lay eggs to make more grasshoppers

How Do Organisms Affect Their Environment?

1 Los Angeles, California, is one of the most air-polluted cities in the United States. On any given day, smog can be seen as a brown haze over the city, as shown in the picture. *Smog* is a word that was created by combining the words *smoke* and *fog*.

What activity would be the **best** way to help reduce the smog in the city?

Ⓐ Recycle old oil.

Ⓑ Pick up roadside trash.

Ⓒ Recycle plastic bottles.

Ⓓ Use public transportation.

2 A pond is a small, enclosed body of fresh water that can be rich in wildlife such as frogs, tadpoles, salamanders, and more. One year, the area around a pond gets very little rainfall, and the pond becomes smaller. Which organism will probably be harmed the **most** by the decrease in the pond's size?

Ⓕ fish   Ⓗ grass

Ⓖ trees   Ⓘ insects

3 Lamar is researching the rainforest. He learned that the rainforest once covered 14% of Earth's land surface; now it covers only 6% because of deforestation. Deforestation is the removal of tress from an area. What is the **most** harmful effect of cutting down so many trees?

Ⓐ more places for animal habitats

Ⓑ an increase in the amount of rain

Ⓒ too much carbon dioxide in the air

Ⓓ not enough room for building houses

4 Casey is making a list of major events that might happen in an ecosystem. He classifies each event as helpful or harmful to the large animals living there. Which of these events would be **helpful** to those animals?

Ⓕ decrease in habitat

Ⓖ increase in temperature

Ⓗ decrease in water supply

Ⓘ increase in number of prey

5 A construction company clears a large section of land in the city where Kobe lives. They plan to build a new subdivision there. Part of the area is wetland where many types of birds, fish, mice, and insects live. Which organisms will be harmed the **most** by the destruction of the wetland habitat?

Ⓐ birds   Ⓒ insects

Ⓑ fish   Ⓓ mice

How Do People Affect Their Environment?

1 St. Lucie County in Florida is building a plant that will turn trash into a gas, which will then be used to generate electricity for 50,000 homes. This plant is expected to begin operating by 2011. What can you expect once the new plant is built?

(A) People in St. Lucie County will produce less trash.

(B) People in St. Lucie County will use less electricity.

(C) The amount of trash will decrease.

(D) The amount of trash will increase.

2 A Florida law controls what kind of fertilizers can be sold for lawns. Some of the chemicals in lawn fertilizer can cause water pollution. Where is this kind of water pollution most likely to occur?

(F) ditches along highways

(G) ponds near neighborhoods

(H) swamps near shopping malls

(I) the ocean along the coastlines

3 Visitors to Florida are encouraged to book their hotel stay with a member of the environmentally friendly Florida Green Lodging Program. What would you **most** likely find at a hotel in the program?

(A) recycling bins

(B) plastic dining utensils

(C) several trash dumpsters

(D) large areas covered with lawns

4 In 2004, Florida developed its environmentally friendly Green Lodging Program. In 2008, Florida reported that the program included about 100,000 hotel and motel rooms. Which of these are you **most** likely to find in one of these rooms?

(F) cleaning products found in all homes

(G) cleaning products that contain toxic chemicals

(H) cleaning products that are not environmentally safe

(I) cleaning products that decompose rapidly in the environment

5 The table below lists what officials in Dania Beach, Florida, consider acceptable and unacceptable wastes left outside homes for pickup.

Trash for pickup	Sample items
Acceptable	table refuse, paper, rags, food scraps, bagged grass clippings
Unacceptable	metal, construction debris, flammable materials, liquids

Which item are residents **not** allowed to place in their trash?

(A) meat bones

(B) newspapers

(C) cereal boxes

(D) used motor oil

Organisms and Their Environment

1 Pam and her family enjoy hiking in a forest a few hours from their home. The picture below shows what they see when they arrive at the forest one day.

What is one way that cutting down trees in the forest is helpful?

(A) The amount of pollution in the area will decrease.

(B) The land can be used for farmland or to build houses.

(C) There will be a greater variety of animals in the forest.

(D) The smaller forest will provide better homes for animals.

SC.4.L.17.4

2 Deshad reads a book about the Florida manatee. He learns that the manatee is a threatened species. What is the **greatest** threat to the manatee in Florida?

(F) not enough food

(G) being hit by a motorboat

(H) chemicals in the water

(I) crossing from fresh water into salt water

SC.4.L.17.4

3 Each summer, Rabin and his family take a vacation at an ocean cottage. This year, they learn that they cannot swim in the ocean because of an oil spill. What effect will the oil spill **most** likely have on the environment?

(A) The air near the oil spill will develop smog.

(B) The temperature of the water will decrease.

(C) The number of cloudy days at the shore will increase.

(D) Fish and water birds will become coated with oil and die.

SC.4.L.17.4

4 Recycling is very important to our environment. Which of the following would probably **not** be sent to a recycling center?

(F) soda cans

(G) newspapers

(H) plastic bottles

(I) cans of paint

SC.4.L.17.4

5 Levi visits a park on a school trip. He notices the tulips pictured below. His teacher tells him that the tulips have just started to flower. Which season did Levi **most** likely see the tulips?

(A) fall   (C) spring

(B) winter   (D) summer

SC.4.L.17.1

6 Plants change throughout the year to suit the seasonal conditions. Which of the following would **not** be expected to be seen during the spring?

Ⓕ new buds forming

Ⓖ fruit trees flowering

Ⓗ green leaves growing

Ⓘ colored leaves falling

SC.4.L.17.1

7 The arctic hare has brown fur during warm months. During cold months, the hare's fur changes to white, as shown in the picture below.

What is the **main** advantage of the hare's white fur?

Ⓐ It stops the hare from losing water.

Ⓑ It reduces the amount of food the hare needs.

Ⓒ It helps the hare remain warm.

Ⓓ It is harder for predators to see the hare.

SC.4.L.17.1

8 Dora needs to complete the chart below.

Facts about . . .		
Consumers	Producers	Decomposers

Which statement belongs in the Producers column?

Ⓕ eat plants

Ⓖ eat animals

Ⓗ use photosynthesis

Ⓘ break down dead material

SC.4.L.17.2

9 The picture below shows the Rocky Mountains during the winter.

Ground hogs in the Rocky Mountains often store food in burrows during the fall. What is the **main** reason for this?

Ⓐ There is little food in the winter.

Ⓑ It is too cold to leave the burrow in the winter.

Ⓒ The burrows would fill with snow in the winter.

Ⓓ They are too easily seen by predators in the winter.

SC.4.L.17.1

10 Some organisms break down dead things for food. Which word describes these organisms?

Ⓕ consumers   Ⓗ herbivores

Ⓖ decomposers   Ⓘ producers

SC.4.L.17.2

11 Plants make their own food through a process called photosynthesis. In order for photosynthesis to happen, sunlight is needed. What else is needed for photosynthesis?

Ⓐ water and sugar

Ⓑ oxygen and sugar

Ⓒ water and carbon dioxide

Ⓓ oxygen and carbon dioxide

SC.4.L.17.2

12 The flow chart below shows an incomplete food chain. The arrows show how energy flows from one living thing to the next.

Producer → ?? → Consumer → Decomposer

What word **best** replaces the blank space in the food chain?

(F) carnivore   (H) predator

(G) consumer   (I) producer

SC.4.L.17.2

13 Matt created the food chain below.

Plant → Animal → Animal → Plant

What is wrong with the food chain that Matt drew?

(A) There cannot be more than one animal in a food chain.

(B) Plants are producers, which means they eat only other plants.

(C) Plants are producers, which means they do not eat other living things.

(D) There should not be any plants in a food chain that does not have decomposers.

SC.4.L.17.2

14 People are part of food chains. What is the role of people in a food chain?

(F) carnivore   (H) herbivore

(G) consumer   (I) producer

SC.4.L.17.3

15 Iguanas are lizards that eat plants and insects. What kind of consumer is the iguana?

(A) carnivore   (C) omnivore

(B) herbivore   (D) producer

SC.4.L.17.3

16 The picture below shows a food chain.

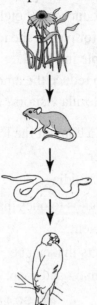

What is the **main** source of energy for this food chain?

(F) hawk

(G) mouse

(H) plants

(I) snake

SC.4.L.17.3

17 In a food chain, the energy moves from organism to organism. Which of the following is the correct order of energy movement in a food chain?

(A) sun, carnivores, predators, herbivores

(B) sun, consumers, predators, producers

(C) sun, producers, herbivores, carnivores

(D) sun, producers, carnivores, herbivores

SC.4.L.17.3

18 Each year, about 40 million people visit Florida. The wastes produced by hotel guests are responsible for part of the total trash produced by people in Florida. Which step would help reduce the amount of trash left by these Florida visitors?

(F) Give every guest a copy of the local Florida newspaper.

(G) Reuse sheets and bedding.

(H) Change all light bulbs to ones that are more energy efficient.

(I) Use only containers that can be refilled with shampoo and soap.

SC.4.L.17.4

19 Many people dispose of solids wastes in compost piles. The compost can then be used as fertilizer. The best items to add to a compost pile are those that will break down rapidly. Such items have a carbon-to-nitrogen ratio of 30 or less.

Approximate Carbon-to-Nitrogen Ratio for Various Materials Commonly Used in Backyard Composts	
Material	**Carbon-to-nitrogen ratio**
Fruit wastes	35
Leaves	60
Sawdust/Wood	600
Table scraps	15

Which item would you expect to break down the fastest in a compost pile?

(A) leftover pieces of wood

(B) leftover broccoli

(C) dry autumn leaves

(D) a branch from a tree

SC.4.N.1.2

20 Recording data is an important part of an experiment. Which data table below would you use to compare how much of different materials decomposed after one week?

(F)

Item	Original color	Color after one week

(G)

Item	Original mass	Mass after one week

(H)

Item	Original shape	Shape after one week

(I)

Item	Original odor	Odor after one week

SC.4.L.17.4

A Food Web

Materials

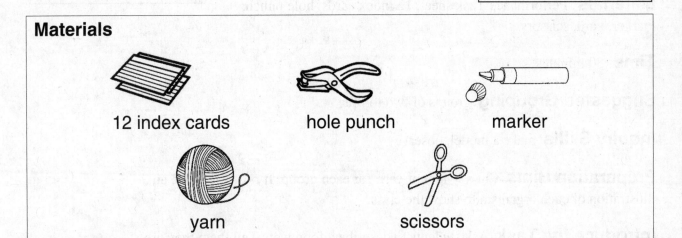

12 index cards   hole punch   marker

yarn   scissors

Procedure

cricket (2)	frog (2)	deer (3)	grass (3)
hawk (4)	mouse (4)	owl (3)	panther (2)
rabbit (4)	shrub (2)	snake (2)	tree (1)

❶ Read the list of organisms. These organisms are part of a food web.

❷ Write the name of each organism on a separate index card.

❸ Look at the list in the box. Each organism has a number next to it.

❹ On each card, punch the number of holes noted next to the name of the organism in the list.

❺ Arrange the cards on your desk so that producers are at the bottom, followed by first-level consumers and second-level consumers, with top-level consumers at the top.

❻ Use yarn to connect the cards to make a food web. Be sure to use all the holes. Compare your food web with those of others in the class. Write a paragraph to describe your food web.

A Food Web

Materials Performance Task sheet, 12 index cards, hole punch, marker, yarn, scissors

Time 30 minutes

Suggested Grouping groups of two to four

Inquiry Skills make a model, observe

Preparation Hints Cut a length of yarn for each group. If possible, have an illustration of each organism to show the class.

Introduce the Task Ask students to describe a food web. Tell them they are going to make a model to show how different organisms interact to form the web. Review the terms *producers, first-level consumers, second-level consumers,* and *top-level consumers.* Model how to mark cards, punch holes, and tie yarn.

Promote Discussion Ask students how they chose the order in which to place the cards to form the web. Ask students to hypothesize about the effect of removing any of the producers or first-level consumers from the web.

Scoring Rubric

Performance Indicators
_____ Works cooperatively with other group members.
_____ Follows written and oral directions.
_____ Makes an accurate model of the food web, using all listed organisms.
_____ Writes a paragraph summarizing the relationship of organisms in the food web.

Observations and Rubric Score
3   **2**   **1**   **0**

1 Within one month, the moon's surface changes as seen from Earth. The entire surface of the moon may be lit, or only a small part may be lit. What causes these changes?

(A) the moon's size

(B) the moon's shape

(C) the moon's revolution

(D) the moon's distance from Earth

SC.4.E.5.2

2 Florida has a variety of natural resources. The illustration below shows how people in Florida use one of these natural resources.

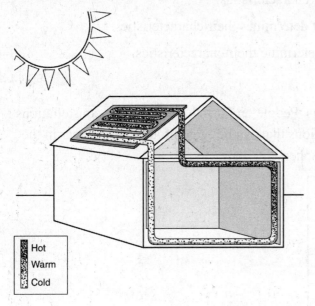

Hot
Warm
Cold

Which natural resource is being used in this illustration?

(F) limestone

(G) oil

(H) phosphate

(I) sunlight

SC.4.E.6.6

3 Jesse and Jacob are identical twins. They have some characteristics that are inherited. They have other characteristics that can be affected by their environment. The table below lists some of their characteristics.

Feature	Jesse	Jacob
eye color	blue	blue
height	6 ft	6 ft 1 in.
skin color	pale	tanned
hair length	short	long

What can you conclude from the information in this table?

Ⓐ Heredity determines all their characteristics.

Ⓑ The environment determines all their characteristics.

Ⓒ Neither heredity nor the environment determines their characteristics.

Ⓓ Both heredity and the environment determine their characteristics.

SC.4.L.16.2

4 Stars form patterns known as constellations. People on Earth have given the constellations names. The table below lists the constellations that can be seen throughout the year in the Northern Hemisphere and Southern Hemisphere.

Season	Northern Hemisphere	Southern Hemisphere
Winter	Orion	Scorpius
Spring	Leo	Pegasus
Summer	Scorpius	Orion
Fall	Pegasus	Leo

What can you conclude from this table?

Ⓕ The constellations that appear depend on the time of night.

Ⓖ The constellations that appear depend on the season of the year.

Ⓗ Different constellations form the same pattern of stars in the sky.

Ⓘ Some constellations appear only in the Northern Hemisphere and others appear only in the Southern Hemisphere.

SC.4.E.5.1

5 During the day, the sun rises in the east and sets in the west. During the night, the moon and stars appear to move across the sky. What makes the sun, moon, and stars appear to move across the sky?

Ⓐ Earth's rotation

Ⓑ the sun's rotation

Ⓒ Earth's revolution

Ⓓ the moon's rotation

SC.4.E.5.4

6 As far back as about 1,000 years ago, people claimed that they had built a perpetual motion machine. They claimed the machine would run forever without having to do anything to it. Scientists know that a perpetual motion machine is impossible to build. The reason is that every machine constantly needs one thing to stay in motion. What does every machine need to stay in motion?

Ⓕ electricity

Ⓖ energy

Ⓗ heat

Ⓘ mass

SC.4.P.10.2

7 Hit a ball and you set it in motion. Pedal a bicycle and you set it in motion. Push a swing and you set it in motion. What must **always** be true of any object that is in motion?

Ⓐ It is moving forward.

Ⓑ It is changing its position.

Ⓒ It is changing its direction.

Ⓓ It is moving at a constant speed.

SC.4.P.12.1

8 Substances can change in different ways. Sometimes they produce new substances. This is called a chemical change. Which is an example of a chemical change?

Ⓕ an ice cube melting

Ⓖ a pencil snapping in two

Ⓗ an eraser getting smaller

Ⓘ a cake baking in an oven

SC.4.P.9.1

9 Plants use sunlight to make their own food. Animals cannot make their own food. The picture below shows the relationship between the sun, plants, and animals. Notice the arrows in this picture.

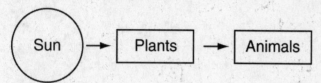

What do the arrows show?

Ⓐ flow of oxygen

Ⓑ flow of energy

Ⓒ flow of nutrients

Ⓓ flow of waste materials

 SC.4.L.17.2

10 Earth revolves around the sun. Look closely at the illustration below, which shows Earth revolving around the sun.

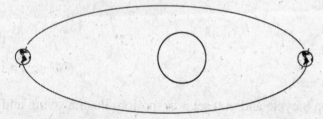

How long will it take for Earth to travel between the two points shown in this illustration?

Ⓕ one week

Ⓖ one month

Ⓗ six months

Ⓘ twelve months

SC.4.E.5.3

11 An erupting volcano can be too dangerous to study up close. As a result, scientists build models to help them understand what they cannot observe directly. This illustration shows an example of one type of model that scientists use.

Which type of model is shown in this illustration?

(A) a photograph

(B) a mental image

(C) a two-dimensional model

(D) a three-dimensional model

SC.4.N.3.1

12 Energy can flow between objects as heat. Look closely at the picture below.

What is one way heat is flowing in the picture?

(F) from the fire to the pot

(G) from the person's hand to the pot

(H) from the person's hand to the fire

(I) from the water in the pot to the fire

SC.4.P.11.1

⓭ Antoine Lavoisier was a French chemist who lived in the 1700s. He developed the law of conservation of mass. He broke a chemical substance into its parts. He found that the individual parts had the same total mass as the original chemical substance.

In science class, Pierre decided to test the law of conservation of mass. He did one test. He broke apart substance AB into its two parts, A and B. The table shows the masses of Part B that Pierre **might** have gotten.

Possible result	Mass of substance AB (g)	Mass of part A (g)	Mass of part B (g)
1	100	93	20
2	100	93	15
3	100	93	7
4	100	93	5

Which possible result shows the mass of part B that Pierre needs to show conservation of mass?

(A) result 1   (C) result 3

(B) result 2   (D) result 4

 SC.4.P.8.3

⓮ Molten rock is called magma. The illustration below shows how magma can rise to Earth's surface.

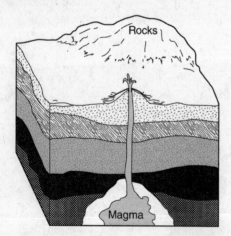

As it cools, magma turns into solid rock on the surface. What type of rock does magma form as it cools?

(F) igneous   (H) sedimentary

(G) metamorphic   (I) fossil

SC.4.E.6.1

15 The coral vine is a plant that grows in many parts of Florida. It is not native to Florida, but was introduced from Mexico. Its beautiful flowers attract butterflies. The coral vine can live where there is air pollution and poor soil. The coral vine also grows very rapidly and crowds out other plants that eventually die. Despite its beauty, scientists are concerned about how the coral vine plant may affect Florida. Which makes the coral vine plant a possible threat to Florida's environment?

(A) It grows in poor soil.

(B) It grows very quickly.

(C) It tolerates air pollution.

(D) It has flowers that attract butterflies.

SC.4.L.17.4

16 Energy is involved when you turn on a lamp. The lamp changes electrical energy into light energy. Which other form of energy is also involved when the lamp is on?

(F) heat energy

(G) solar energy

(H) sound energy

(I) wind energy

SC.4.P.10.1

17 The Florida manatee is very sensitive to temperature changes. As a result, manatees migrate to warmer waters in the winter. They especially like to pass the winter months near energy stations, which discharge warm water into the local waters. Manatees normally rest and feed often. They communicate by squealing under water to show fear, stress, or excitement. Which behavior is an example of a seasonal change in manatees?

(A) squealing when danger is near

(B) being sensitive to temperature changes

(C) spending the winter near energy stations

(D) resting and feeding often during the day

SC.4.L.17.1

18 Florida International University has powerful microscopes. How might these microscopes be used by the Earth Sciences Department at the university?

   (F)   to study the orbit of a planet

   (G)   to look at the craters on the moon

   (H)   to observe the parts of an animal cell

   (I)   to examine the chemical structure of a mineral

SC.4.E.6.5

19 The eastern lubber grasshopper is a common sight in Florida. This grasshopper can get as long as 7 cm. The female grasshopper lays eggs. The eggs hatch into nymphs. Nymphs look like small adults, but without wings. Which statement is **true** about the eastern lubber grasshopper?

   (A)   This grasshopper does not reproduce sexually.

   (B)   This grasshopper can fly shortly after the eggs hatch.

   (C)   This grasshopper goes through complete metamorphosis.

   (D)   This grasshopper goes through incomplete metamorphosis.

SC.4.L.16.4

20 Erik was investigating how rocks can change. He carried out the following procedure.

1. Place several sugar cubes in a jar.
2. Seal the jar and shake it 50 times.
3. Dump the sugar cubes on a piece of black paper.
4. Compare the appearance of the sugar cubes to their original size and shape.

What process was Erik studying?

   (F)   deposition

   (G)   erosion

   (H)   sedimentation

   (I)   weathering

SC.4.E.6.4

21 Water is a very common substance. Yet, water has some unusual properties. For example, you can find water in all three states of matter at the same time. You can take ice cubes from a freezer and put them in a glass. You can put water from a faucet in a pot, and boil it on the stove. Where will you find water as a liquid turning into a gas?

(A) in the glass

(B) on the stove

(C) in the freezer

(D) from the faucet

SC.4.P.8.2

22 During a storm, you can sometimes hear thunder. The sound of thunder is produced by vibrations. What vibrates to make the sound of thunder?

(F) the air

(G) the clouds

(H) the ground

(I) the lightning bolt

SC.4.P.10.3

23 Sandra is investigating the physical properties of matter. The physical property she is studying is mass. She uses a balance to measure the mass of four objects. Which balance shows the object with the **most** mass?

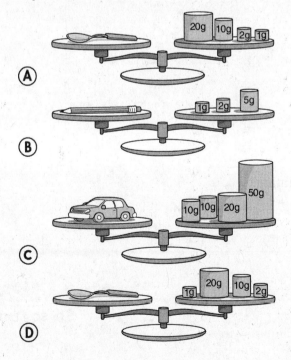

SC.4.P.8.1

24 Mr. Chu asked his science class what would happen to the mass of a pencil if he smashed it into pieces. The students said that the mass of the pieces added together would be the same as the mass of the pencil. What evidence would these students need to support their claim?

F The mass of all the tiny pieces was less than the mass of the object.

G The mass of all the tiny pieces was equal to the mass of the object.

H The mass of all the tiny pieces was greater than the mass of the object.

I The mass of all the tiny pieces was too small to be measured with a balance.

SC.4.N.1.4, SC.4.P.8.3

25 Madison's science class is studying how energy can move things. The teacher talks about sources of energy. Which of the following statements about energy is correct?

A Energy is a limited resource.

B Moving air is a source of energy.

C Wind can replace all other energy resources.

D Sources of energy must come from the ground.

SC.4.P.10.4

26 People who visit an aquarium often enjoy seeing the dolphin show. The picture below shows something a dolphin may do during one of these shows.

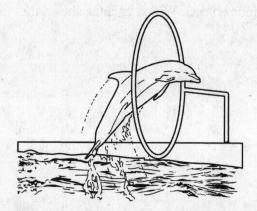

What type of behavior is this dolphin demonstrating?

F learned, only

G hereditary, only

H both hereditary and learned

I neither hereditary nor learned

SC.4.L.16.3

27 One physical property of a mineral is its hardness. A harder mineral can scratch a softer mineral. The table below shows a scale that rates the hardness of minerals. For example, diamond, with a hardness rating of 10, is the hardest mineral. Diamond can scratch corundum, which has a hardness rating of 9. However, corundum cannot scratch diamond.

Mineral	Hardness rating
talc	1
gypsum	2
calcite	3
fluorite	4
apatite	5
orthoclase	6
quartz	7
topaz	8
corundum	9
diamond	10

A mineral called beryl can scratch quartz but not topaz. What is the hardness rating of beryl?

(A) 9.5
(B) 8.5
(C) 7.5
(D) 6.5

SC.4.E.6.2

28 Flowering plants use sexual reproduction to produce new plants. Sexual reproduction in plants involves several processes, including the one shown in the picture below.

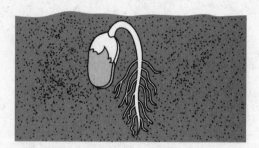

Which process is shown in this picture?

(F) pollination

(G) fertilization

(H) seed dispersal

(I) seed germination

SC.4.L.16.1

29 Scientists are always searching for answers to explain how the natural world works. Their explanations must be based on evidence. What do scientists use as evidence to support their explanations?

(A) conclusions

(B) data

(C) hypotheses

(D) theories

SC.4.N.1.7

There are many different types of scientists. For example, some scientists study the structure of Earth, while other scientists study living things. All scientists, including the one shown in this illustration, follow the same general pattern in their work.

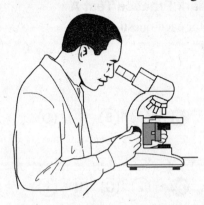

Which represents the correct sequence of steps that scientists follow in their work?

Ⓕ conduct an investigation ‣ ask a question ‣ record and display data ‣ draw conclusions

Ⓖ record and display data ‣ conduct an investigation ‣ ask a question ‣ draw conclusions

Ⓗ draw conclusions ‣ conduct an investigation ‣ record and display data ‣ ask a question

Ⓘ ask a question ‣ conduct an investigation ‣ record and display data ‣ draw conclusions

 SC.4.N.1.1

PLEASE NOTE
- Use only a no. 2 pencil
- Example: Ⓐ ● Ⓒ Ⓓ
- Erase changes COMPLETELY.

Florida Benchmark Practice Test A
Mark one answer for each question.

❶ Ⓐ Ⓑ Ⓒ Ⓓ   ⓫ Ⓐ Ⓑ Ⓒ Ⓓ   ㉑ Ⓐ Ⓑ Ⓒ Ⓓ

❷ Ⓕ Ⓖ Ⓗ Ⓘ   ⓬ Ⓕ Ⓖ Ⓗ Ⓘ   ㉒ Ⓕ Ⓖ Ⓗ Ⓘ

❸ Ⓐ Ⓑ Ⓒ Ⓓ   ⓭ Ⓐ Ⓑ Ⓒ Ⓓ   ㉓ Ⓐ Ⓑ Ⓒ Ⓓ

❹ Ⓕ Ⓖ Ⓗ Ⓘ   ⓮ Ⓕ Ⓖ Ⓗ Ⓘ   ㉔ Ⓕ Ⓖ Ⓗ Ⓘ

❺ Ⓐ Ⓑ Ⓒ Ⓓ   ⓯ Ⓐ Ⓑ Ⓒ Ⓓ   ㉕ Ⓐ Ⓑ Ⓒ Ⓓ

❻ Ⓕ Ⓖ Ⓗ Ⓘ   ⓰ Ⓕ Ⓖ Ⓗ Ⓘ   ㉖ Ⓕ Ⓖ Ⓗ Ⓘ

❼ Ⓐ Ⓑ Ⓒ Ⓓ   ⓱ Ⓐ Ⓑ Ⓒ Ⓓ   ㉗ Ⓐ Ⓑ Ⓒ Ⓓ

❽ Ⓕ Ⓖ Ⓗ Ⓘ   ⓲ Ⓕ Ⓖ Ⓗ Ⓘ   ㉘ Ⓕ Ⓖ Ⓗ Ⓘ

❾ Ⓐ Ⓑ Ⓒ Ⓓ   ⓳ Ⓐ Ⓑ Ⓒ Ⓓ   ㉙ Ⓐ Ⓑ Ⓒ Ⓓ

❿ Ⓕ Ⓖ Ⓗ Ⓘ   ⓴ Ⓕ Ⓖ Ⓗ Ⓘ   ㉚ Ⓕ Ⓖ Ⓗ Ⓘ

1 The different ways the moon looks as it orbits Earth are called phases. One phase is called a full moon. During a full moon, the entire surface of the moon as seen from Earth is in sunlight. How are Earth, the moon, and sun arranged during a full moon?

Ⓐ The sun is between Earth and the moon.

Ⓑ The moon is between Earth and the sun.

Ⓒ Earth is on the side of the moon in darkness.

Ⓓ Earth is located between the sun and the moon.

SC.4.E.5.2

2 A food chain shows how energy flows in a community of plants and animals. The pyramid below shows what happens to energy as it flows up through a food chain.

This food chain consists of plants → mice →snakes → hawk.

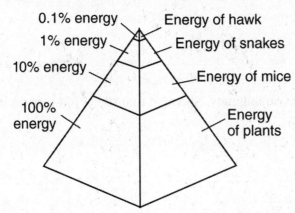

What can you conclude from this picture?

Ⓕ The amount of energy decreases as it flows through a food chain.

Ⓖ The amount of energy increases as it passes through a food chain.

Ⓗ The amount of energy is the same at the beginning and end of a food chain.

Ⓘ The amount of energy is greatest when the last stage of a food chain is reached.

SC.4.L.17.3

3 Two instruments that were aboard the Hubble Space Telescope are expected to become part of a permanent collection at the National Air and Space Museum in Washington, DC. Both instruments were on the Hubble Space Telescope for 15 years. However, the instruments were replaced when they stopped working. What did these two instruments help the Hubble Space Telescope do?

(A) provide information about the weather on Earth

(B) take close-up images of distant objects in the universe

(C) measure the gases that make up Earth's atmosphere

(D) track the space shuttle and its crew as they orbit Earth

SC.4.E.6.5

4 One form of energy is heat. Heat always flows between objects. What happens to the object into which heat flows?

(F) Its temperature falls.

(G) Its temperature rises.

(H) It changes from a liquid into a solid.

(I) It changes from a gas into a liquid.

SC.4.P.11.1

5 Mariana is interested in doing an investigation on magnets. She read that she could turn an iron nail into a magnet as shown in this illustration.

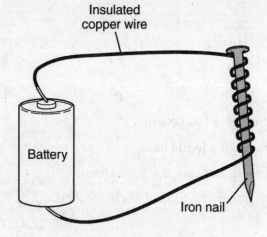

What must happen to show that Mariana's investigation worked?

(A) The copper wire conducts electricity.

(B) The copper wire becomes too hot to touch.

(C) The iron nail attracts some metal paper clips.

(D) The iron nail attracts some plastic paper clips.

SC.4.N.1.5

6 People build homes with many different materials. Builders often put fiberglass in walls to insulate the homes. Why may builders use fiberglass to insulate walls?

(F) Fiberglass conducts heat.

(G) Fiberglass does not conduct heat.

(H) Fiberglass prevents moisture from entering the house.

(I) Fiberglass blocks sunlight and keeps the house cooler.

SC.4.P.11.2

7 Animals, including humans, cannot make their own food. Animals need to get energy from something else so they can survive and grow. How do animals get the energy they need?

(A) from the sun

(B) from plants, only

(C) from other animals, only

(D) from both plants and other animals

SC.4.L.17.2

8 Imagine that you are hunting for fossils. Which type of rock would you be investigating?

(F) igneous

(G) magma

(H) metamorphic

(I) sedimentary

SC.4.E.6.1

9 Humans need resources found on Earth. Humans use some of these resources to generate electricity. The figure below shows which resources humans use to generate electricity.

Energy Resources

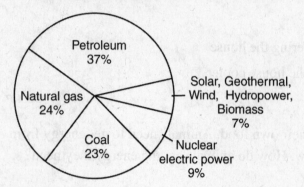

Which resource in this figure is considered a renewable resource?

Ⓐ coal

Ⓑ petroleum

Ⓒ solar

Ⓓ nuclear power

SC.4.E.6.3

10 Sexual reproduction in flowering plants involves several processes. Sometimes animals have a role in these processes. In which two of these processes do animals play a role?

Ⓕ pollination and fertilization

Ⓖ pollination and seed dispersal

Ⓗ seed dispersal and fertilization

Ⓘ seed germination and seed dispersal

SC.4.L.16.1

11 Water can exist as a solid, liquid, or gas. Mei left an orange on the kitchen table for two hours. Which state of water is **best** to use for cooling Mei's warm orange?

Ⓐ gas

Ⓑ solid

Ⓒ liquid

Ⓓ both gas and liquid

SC.4.P.8.2

⑫   Water can play a role in both the weathering and the erosion of rocks. Look closely at the illustrations below.

A

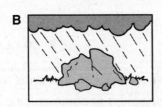

B

C

D

Which letter represents erosion?

Ⓕ   A

Ⓖ   B

Ⓗ   C

Ⓘ   D

SC.4.E.6.4

⑬   If you look up at the night sky long enough, the stars will appear to move across the sky. What is responsible for making the stars appear to move across the sky at night?

Ⓐ   Earth's revolution

Ⓑ   Earth's rotation on its axis

Ⓒ   Earth's position in its orbit

Ⓓ   Earth's distance from the sun

SC.4.E.5.1

14 The apple snail is an important part of food chains found in Florida's marshes. The apple snail is also part of many home aquariums. One reason people like to place them in fish tanks is that the apple snail is the biggest living freshwater snail on Earth. However, people who have snails in their fish tanks should never release them into local ponds or rivers. What is the reason?

(F) Apple snails will not survive in the ponds and rivers.

(G) Apple snails will threaten life in the ponds and rivers.

(H) Apple snails will not grow as large in ponds and rivers.

(I) Apple snails will no longer be part of food chains in Florida's marshes.

SC.4.L.17.4

15 Some human behaviors involve communication. For example, Jessica may wave her arms to get her friend's attention. However, humans mainly depend on their voices to communicate. Which example of vocal communication is determined **only** by heredity?

(A) a baby crying at night

(B) a student asking a question

(C) a teacher explaining the answer

(D) a teenager talking on a cell phone

SC.4.L.16.3

16 Jessica takes care of her house and yard. She has to do something with the plant and animal wastes she collects. The picture below shows where she puts the waste materials.

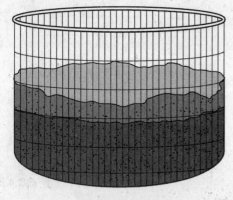

Compost pile

How is the object in the picture an example of a place where chemical changes occur?

(F) The wastes change their mass.

(G) The wastes change into completely new substances.

(H) The wastes change into materials with the same properties.

(I) The wastes change their physical properties, such as shape.

SC.4.P.9.1

17 Scientists are often creative when they design their experiments.

What is one way a scientist can be creative when designing an experiment?

Ⓐ A scientist prepares all the materials in advance.

Ⓑ A scientist finds the procedure from a lab manual.

Ⓒ A scientist uses supplies borrowed from another lab.

Ⓓ A scientist decides to rearrange the steps used before.

SC.4.N.1.8

18 On NASA's 50th anniversary, Florida's *Sun Sentinel* reported, "It is to Florida's benefit that the space program retains its vitality, and its Cape Canaveral launch pad." How does NASA directly benefit the state of Florida?

Ⓕ NASA launches space shuttles.

Ⓖ NASA trains astronauts for space travel.

Ⓗ NASA provides jobs for local communities.

Ⓘ NASA makes discoveries about our universe.

SC.4.E.5.5

19 Energy exists in different forms. Look closely at the table below.

Source	Noise level
rock concert	High
diesel truck	Moderate
vacuum cleaner	Moderate
bedroom at night	Low

Which form of energy do the sources in the table produce?

Ⓐ electrical

Ⓑ heat

Ⓒ light

Ⓓ sound

SC.4.P.10.1

20 Liu did the following experiment in her science class.

1. Sprinkle some rice on a paper plate.
2. Place the plate on top of a speaker.
3. Turn on the music.
4. Watch the rice dance to the music.

What can Liu conclude based on her observations?

Ⓕ Energy can cause motion.

Ⓖ Energy is in foods, such as rice.

Ⓗ Energy can exist in the form of light.

Ⓘ Energy is used to make new substances.

SC.4.P.10.2

21 Caitlin was studying speed. She measured the distance a toy car traveled. She recorded her data in the following table.

Trial	Distance (m)	Time (sec)
1	2	10
2	4	10
3	6	10
4	8	10

In which trial did the car have the **fastest** speed?

(A) trial 1

(B) trial 2

(C) trial 3

(D) trial 4

SC.4.P.12.2

22 In science class, Carlos is studying physical properties of matter. The matter he will investigate is water. He made the table below for entering his observations.

Physical property	Description
attraction to magnets	
hardness	
odor	
shape	

For which physical property will Carlos write a description, rather than just writing "no"?

(F) attraction to magnets

(G) hardness

(H) odor

(I) shape

SC.4.P.8.1

23 The picture below shows two plants. Plant 1 was grown in the dark. Plant 2 was grown in the light.

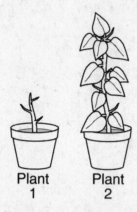

Plant
1

Plant
2

What can you conclude about the growth of these plants?

Ⓐ The environment can affect physical features.

Ⓑ The environment determines all physical features.

Ⓒ The environment plays no role in the growth of plants.

Ⓓ The environment determines which structures a plant will have.

SC.4.L.16.2

24 Earth is constantly moving in space. What will happen between noon today and noon tomorrow?

Ⓕ Earth will complete 1 rotation.

Ⓖ Earth will complete 7 rotations.

Ⓗ Earth will complete about 30 rotations.

Ⓘ Earth will complete about 365 rotations.

SC.4.E.5.3

25 When you travel in a car, both you and the car are in motion. When you go to an amusement park, you can be in motion, too. The picture below shows an amusement park ride in motion.

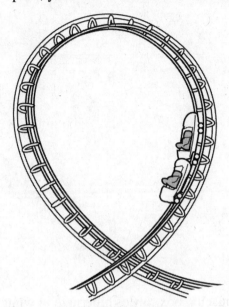

Which statement is **true** about the object in motion in the picture?

Ⓐ The object is changing only its position.

Ⓑ The object is changing only its direction.

Ⓒ The object is changing both its position and direction.

Ⓓ The object is changing neither its position nor direction.

SC.4.P.12.1

26 Both Earth and the moon rotate and revolve. The table below lists about how long it takes for these rotations and revolutions.

Object	Rotation	Revolution
Earth	24 hr	365 days
moon	27 days	29 days

What can you conclude from this table?

Ⓕ Earth takes longer than the moon to complete one rotation.

Ⓖ The moon takes longer than Earth to complete one revolution.

Ⓗ The moon takes almost the same time to complete one rotation and one revolution.

Ⓘ Earth completes one rotation in the same time it takes the moon to complete one revolution.

SC.4.E.5.4

27 Box turtles may live for 100 years. They live in open woodlands, pastures, and marshy meadows.

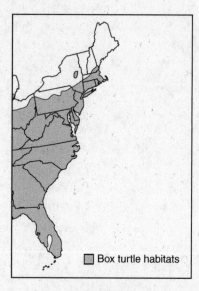

Box turtle habitats

In Florida, box turtles are active year-round. In Massachusetts, box turtles hibernate in winter. What does this illustrate **best** about box turtles in Florida and Massachusetts?

(A) life expectancy

(B) winter behavior

(C) food preferences

(D) habitat preferences

SC.4.L.17.1

28 Florida supplies about 75% of one of the ingredients found in fertilizers used in this country. What is the ingredient?

(F) oil

(G) phosphate

(H) silicon

(I) water

SC.4.E.6.6

29 In the 1200s, sailors used a type of rock called lodestone as a compass. They hung the lodestone on the end of a string. The sailors knew that the lodestone always pointed north. How was the lodestone acting?

(A) as a magnet

(B) as an insulator

(C) as a conductor

(D) as a source of energy

SC.4.P.8.4

30 Mrs. Alvarez divided her science class into four groups to study the motion of a toy car. Each group drew a graph to show the distance that the toy car traveled over a period of time. However, one group of students did not draw their graph correctly because their graph shows that the car did not move at all. Which graph did this group draw?

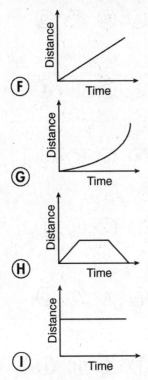

(F)

(G)

(H)

(I)

SC.4.N.1.2, SC.4.P.12.2

Answer Sheet

PLEASE NOTE

- Use only a no. 2 pencil
- Example: (A) ● (C) (D)
- Erase changes COMPLETELY.

Florida Benchmark Practice Test B
Mark one answer for each question.

❶ (A) (B) (C) (D)   ⑪ (A) (B) (C) (D)   ㉑ (A) (B) (C) (D)

❷ (F) (G) (H) (I)   ⑫ (F) (G) (H) (I)   ㉒ (F) (G) (H) (I)

❸ (A) (B) (C) (D)   ⑬ (A) (B) (C) (D)   ㉓ (A) (B) (C) (D)

❹ (F) (G) (H) (I)   ⑭ (F) (G) (H) (I)   ㉔ (F) (G) (H) (I)

❺ (A) (B) (C) (D)   ⑮ (A) (B) (C) (D)   ㉕ (A) (B) (C) (D)

❻ (F) (G) (H) (I)   ⑯ (F) (G) (H) (I)   ㉖ (F) (G) (H) (I)

❼ (A) (B) (C) (D)   ⑰ (A) (B) (C) (D)   ㉗ (A) (B) (C) (D)

❽ (F) (G) (H) (I)   ⑱ (F) (G) (H) (I)   ㉘ (F) (G) (H) (I)

❾ (A) (B) (C) (D)   ⑲ (A) (B) (C) (D)   ㉙ (A) (B) (C) (D)

❿ (F) (G) (H) (I)   ⑳ (F) (G) (H) (I)   ㉚ (F) (G) (H) (I)

1 Luis challenges Reba to describe the physical properties of an object while she is blindfolded. Which physical property will Reba be able to describe **best**?

(A) color

(B) mass

(C) texture

(D) volume

SC.4.P.8.1

2 Experiments often involve both observations and inferences. Georgia plotted the results of a speed experiment she did. Look closely at the graph that she drew.

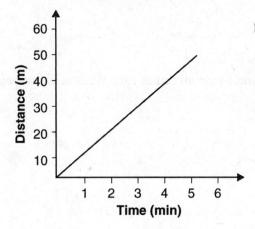

Distance vs. Time

At what time must Georgia make an inference about the distance the object traveled?

(F) 1 min

(G) 2 min

(H) 5 min

(I) 6 min

SC.4.N.1.6

3 Mr. Poloski asked his science class to show how energy flows through a community of plants and animals. He made three signs and asked three students to choose a sign. The table below shows what sign each student picked.

Student	Sign
Miguel	consumer
Elisa	sun
John	producer

Mr. Poloski asked the students to line up to show how energy flows through a community.

Which shows the **correct** order as to how the students should line up?

(A) Elisa → Miguel → John

(B) Miguel → John → Elisa

(C) John → Elisa → Miguel

(D) Elisa → John → Miguel

SC.4.L.17.3

4 Earth moves through space by spinning on its axis and by orbiting the sun. What will happen between January 1, 2012 and January 1, 2013?

(F) Earth will complete 1 rotation.

(G) Earth will complete 12 rotations.

(H) Earth will complete 1 revolution.

(I) Earth will complete 365 revolutions.

SC.4.E.5.3

5 Water can move small rocks quickly along the bottom of a fast-flowing river. As they move, the rocks bump into and scrape against each other. Some of these rocks may settle at the bottom of the river as the water slows down. Here the rocks may become covered with sediments that pile up. Which of the following represents the weathering of these rocks?

(A) the bumping and scraping of the rocks

(B) the movement of the rocks along the river

(C) the settling of the rocks at the bottom of the river

(D) the covering of the rocks with sediments that pile up

SC.4.E.6.4

6 The zebra longwing butterfly is the state insect of Florida. The picture below shows its life cycle.

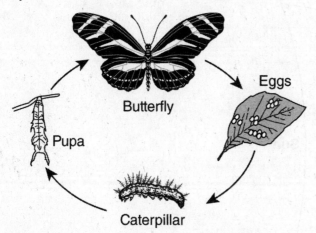

Butterfly

Eggs

Pupa

Caterpillar

What does the picture tell you about the life cycle of the zebra longwing butterfly?

(F) It goes through three stages.

(G) It goes through complete metamorphosis.

(H) It goes through incomplete metamorphosis.

(I) It goes through its life cycle in three weeks.

SC.4.L.16.4

7 Light travels through space and strikes Earth. Sounds do not travel through space to reach Earth. Why can light travel through space, but sound cannot?

(A) There is no energy in space.

(B) Sound does not travel as energy.

(C) Sound does not travel as fast as light.

(D) There is no matter in space to vibrate.

SC.4.P.10 .3

8 The movements of Earth and the moon are related. Look closely at the illustration below.

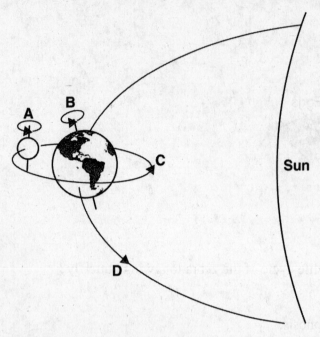

Which letter represents the movement that takes the **longest** amount of time?

Ⓕ A

Ⓖ B

Ⓗ C

Ⓘ D

SC.4.E.5.4

9 One of Florida's natural resources is found in the bedrock on which the state rests. Which material makes up this bedrock?

Ⓐ limestone

Ⓑ phosphate

Ⓒ sand

Ⓓ silicon

SC.4.E.6.6

10 Bobbi did an experiment that involved holding a metal wire in the flame of a burning candle. She included the drawing below in her report.

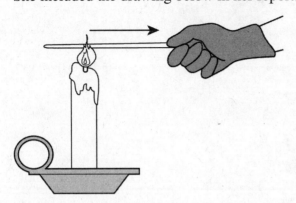

Why did Bobbi put the arrow in her drawing?

(F) to show where she was standing

(G) to show how the candle got smaller

(H) to show that the candle was burning

(I) to show the metal wire was a conductor

SC.4.P.11.2

11 Mercury is a poison that can affect a person's health. Mercury gets into the environment in several ways. One way is by the dumping of industrial wastes into rivers and lakes. Once it is in the water, mercury can enter a food chain. The mercury builds up as it works its way through a food chain. The organisms at the end of the food chain will have the highest level of mercury. The picture below shows mercury being dumped into a lake.

Which organism in the picture will have the **highest** level of mercury?

(A) plants

(B) small fish

(C) large fish

(D) person fishing

SC.4.L.17.4

12 The illustration below shows an astronaut performing an extravehicular activity. It is known as a space walk.

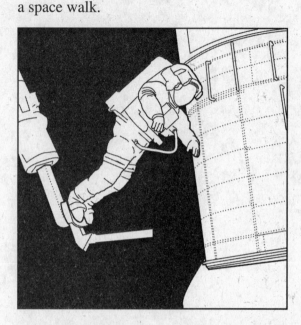

In 1984, NASA astronaut Kathryn Sullivan became the first American woman to walk in space. In 1995, NASA astronaut Dr. Bernard Harris, Jr. became the first African-American to walk in space. Franklin Chang-Diaz, the first U.S. Hispanic astronaut, holds the record for most space walks. From this information, what can you conclude about how NASA has affected the Florida community?

(F) NASA has attracted tourists to Florida.

(G) NASA has developed land areas in Florida.

(H) NASA has contributed to Florida's economy.

(I) NASA has promoted cultural diversity in Florida.

SC.4.E.5.5

13 Look outside your house and you may see an iron hinge rusting. Look inside your house and you may see vegetables cooking in a pot on the stove. You might not think that rusting and cooking have anything in common. However, they do. What do both rusting and cooking have in common?

(A) They both involve physical changes.

(B) They both involve chemical changes.

(C) They both involve magnetic materials.

(D) They both involve nonmagnetic materials.

SC.4.P.9.1

14 The moon orbits Earth. This orbit causes the moon to look different over the course of about a month. These differences are called phases. One phase is called a full moon. Look closely at the table below.

Moon Phases—Summer 2005				
Month	New Moon	First Quarter	Full Moon	Third Quarter
June	6	15	22	28
July	6	14	21	28
August	5	13	19	26
September	4	11	18	25

What can you conclude about a full moon?

(F) A full moon always occurs after a first quarter moon.

(G) A full moon always occurs on the 5th day of the month.

(H) A full moon always occurs before the first quarter moon.

(I) A full moon only occurs in the summer months.

SC.4.E.5.2

15 The Florida sweetgum tree can grow to a height of 150 ft. The tree gets its name from the fact that early settlers peeled the bark and scraped the sap to use as chewing gum. The tree is easily identified by its leaves, which are shaped like stars. In fall, the leaves turn red, orange, purple, and yellow. Which is a seasonal change in the sweetgum tree?

(A) growth to a height of 150 ft

(B) presence of star-shaped leaves

(C) production of a chewy, gummy sap

(D) leaves turning from green into various colors

SC.4.L.17.1

16 Magnets come in different shapes. Some magnets have a shape like the letter *U* or a horseshoe. How could you tell where the north-seeking pole is on a horseshoe magnet?

(F) Bring the magnet near a piece of paper.

(G) Bring the magnet near any nonmagnetic material.

(H) Bring the magnet near the pole of another magnet.

(I) Bring the magnet near some paper clips on a piece of paper.

SC.4.P.8.4

17 People learn about science by watching television and reading magazines. Which magazine title reveals what life scientists focus on in their work?

(A) *Nature*

(B) *Discover*

(C) *Science News*

(D) *Scientific American*

SC.4.N.2.1

18 A deer is eating grass. A mouse is eating seeds. What can you conclude from this information?

(F) The deer gets its energy from the mouse.

(G) The mouse gets its energy from the grass.

(H) The grass and seeds store energy for animals.

(I) The deer and mouse can produce the foods they need.

SC.4.L.17.2

19 Tools have helped scientists to gain a better understanding of our natural world. This is true even for the first scientists. For example, in the early 1600s, Galileo used the instrument shown below to study space.

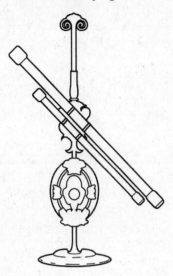

What did Galileo discover by using this instrument?

Ⓐ Earth's moon

Ⓑ water on the moon

Ⓒ phases of the moon

Ⓓ moons circling Jupiter

SC.4.E.6.5

20 Andrew observed the change of temperature of an object. Its temperature went from 40 °C to 20 °C. What is Andrew's **most** likely conclusion about the object?

Ⓕ It is melting

Ⓖ It is getting larger.

Ⓗ It is changing its color.

Ⓘ It is losing energy as heat.

SC.4.P.11.1

21 Minerals have various physical properties. The illustration below shows a tool that is used to test a physical property of minerals.

What physical property of a mineral is tested using this tool?

Ⓐ cleavage

Ⓑ color

Ⓒ luster

Ⓓ streak

SC.4.E.6.2

22 Energy can cause motion. Which of the following is an example of energy causing something to move?

Ⓕ reading a book

Ⓖ watching television

Ⓗ pushing a toy truck down a hill

Ⓘ sitting on a chair

SC.4.P.10 .2

23 You find the speed of a moving object by measuring the distance it travels in a unit of time. The graph below shows how far a scooter can move.

Scooter Movement

How far will the scooter move in 6 sec?

Ⓐ 55 m

Ⓑ 60 m

Ⓒ 65 m

Ⓓ 70 m

SC.4.P.12.2

24 A scientist may perform experiments in a laboratory to find an answer to a question. Another scientist may work outdoors making observations to find an answer to a question. What do both scientists have in common?

Ⓕ They are following the same method in their work.

Ⓖ They are collecting evidence to reach a conclusion.

Ⓗ They are challenging the opinions of other scientists.

Ⓘ They are comparing their findings with other scientists.

SC.4.N.1.3

25 Animals can move and inhabit a large geographic area. Plants cannot move. What process helps plants inhabit a large geographic area?

Ⓐ pollination

Ⓑ fertilization

Ⓒ seed dispersal

Ⓓ seed germination

SC.4.L.16.1

26 If you stare closely at the night sky, the stars will seem to move. However, there is one star that will not appear to move no matter how long you stare at it. Look at the illustration below.

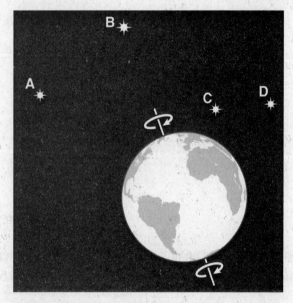

Which star will appear to remain in the same position in the night sky?

Ⓕ star A

Ⓖ star B

Ⓗ star C

Ⓘ star D

SC.4.E.5.1

27 When wood burns in a fireplace, the ashes are left. The gases escape up the chimney. Suppose you could trap the gases. What would you find about the mass of the wood?

(A) It is less than the mass of the ashes and gases.

(B) It is the same as the mass of the ashes and gases.

(C) It is greater than the mass of the ashes and gases.

(D) It is the same as the mass of the gases that escaped.

SC.4.P.8.3

28 Moving water can be a source of energy. For example, a certain type of energy station uses the energy from moving water to generate electricity. Which type of energy station is this?

(F) nuclear

(G) fossil fuel

(H) geothermal

(I) hydroelectric

SC.4.P.10.4

29 The South Florida Natural Resources Center is a division of Everglades National Park. What do you think this resource center does?

(A) promotes tourists to visit Florida

(B) warns local residents of hurricanes

(C) provides information on Florida's crops

(D) educates people about the local environment

SC.4.E.6.3

30 Ms. Leon asked Alicia to describe four things she did that morning. Alicia said that she rode her bicycle to school, spoke Spanish with her friend, jumped when the fire alarm sounded, and finished her science and math homework. What did Alicia do that was instinctive behavior?

(F) rode her bicycle to school

(G) spoke Spanish with her friend

(H) jumped when the fire alarm sounded

(I) finished her science and math homework

SC.4.L.16.3

PLEASE NOTE
- Use only a no. 2 pencil
- Example: (A) ● (C) (D)
- Erase changes COMPLETELY.

Florida Benchmark Practice Test C
Mark one answer for each question.

1 (A) (B) (C) (D) **11** (A) (B) (C) (D) **21** (A) (B) (C) (D)

2 (F) (G) (H) (I) **12** (F) (G) (H) (I) **22** (F) (G) (H) (I)

3 (A) (B) (C) (D) **13** (A) (B) (C) (D) **23** (A) (B) (C) (D)

4 (F) (G) (H) (I) **14** (F) (G) (H) (I) **24** (F) (G) (H) (I)

5 (A) (B) (C) (D) **15** (A) (B) (C) (D) **25** (A) (B) (C) (D)

6 (F) (G) (H) (I) **16** (F) (G) (H) (I) **26** (F) (G) (H) (I)

7 (A) (B) (C) (D) **17** (A) (B) (C) (D) **27** (A) (B) (C) (D)

8 (F) (G) (H) (I) **18** (F) (G) (H) (I) **28** (F) (G) (H) (I)

9 (A) (B) (C) (D) **19** (A) (B) (C) (D) **29** (A) (B) (C) (D)

10 (F) (G) (H) (I) **20** (F) (G) (H) (I) **30** (F) (G) (H) (I)

Unit 1 Studying Science

Lesson 1 Quiz, p. AG 1
1. B
2. F
3. A
4. F
5. A

Lesson 2 Quiz, p. AG 2
1. A
2. G
3. D
4. F
5. C

Lesson 3 Quiz, p. AG 3
1. C
2. H
3. D
4. G
5. D

Lesson 4 Quiz, p. AG 4
1. A
2. H
3. D
4. H
5. C

Lesson 5 Quiz, p. AG 5
1. B
2. F
3. A
4. G
5. D

Lesson 6 Quiz, p. AG 6
1. A
2. I
3. A
4. F
5. D

Unit 1 Benchmark Test, pp. AG 7–10
1. C
2. I
3. C
4. F
5. C
6. I
7. C
8. H
9. B
10. H
11. B
12. H
13. D
14. I
15. B
16. G
17. C
18. I
19. F
20. B

Unit 2 Earth's Place in Space

Lesson 1 Quiz, p. AG 13
1. A
2. I
3. C
4. I
5. A

Lesson 2 Quiz, p. AG 14
1. C
2. H
3. D
4. I
5. D

Lesson 3 Quiz, p. AG 15
1. C
2. I
3. D
4. F
5. A

Lesson 4 Quiz, p. AG 16
1. B
2. G
3. C
4. I
5. D

Unit 2 Benchmark Test, pp. AG 17–20
1. D
2. I
3. A
4. H
5. A
6. I
7. C
8. G
9. D
10. H
11. C
12. H
13. D
14. G
15. D
16. H
17. B
18. G
19. B
20. I

Unit 3 Rocks, Minerals, and Resources

Lesson 1 Quiz, p. AG 23
1. B
2. I
3. A
4. H
5. A

Lesson 2 Quiz, p. AG 24
1. C
2. G
3. D
4. F
5. B

Lesson 3 Quiz, p. AG 25
1. B
2. H
3. A
4. G
5. C

Lesson 4 Quiz, p. AG 26

1. D
2. G
3. D
4. H
5. B

Lesson 5 Quiz, p. AG 27

1. C
2. I
3. A
4. I
5. D

Unit 3 Benchmark Test, pp. AG 28–31

1. D
2. F
3. C
4. I
5. C
6. F
7. B
8. H
9. C
10. H
11. C
12. F
13. D
14. F
15. A
16. I
17. C
18. G
19. C
20. G

Unit 4 Matter and Its Properties

Lesson 1 Quiz, p. AG 34

1. D
2. I
3. C
4. I
5. C

Lesson 2 Quiz, p. AG 35

1. D
2. H
3. C
4. H
5. D

Lesson 3 Quiz, p. AG 36

1. B
2. F
3. B
4. G
5. B

Lesson 4 Quiz, p. AG 37

1. A
2. H
3. A
4. H
5. A

Lesson 5 Quiz, p. AG 38

1. B
2. F
3. B
4. I
5. C

Lesson 6 Quiz, p. AG 39

1. C
2. H
3. D
4. F
5. A

Unit 4 Benchmark Test, pp. AG 40–43

1. D
2. F
3. D
4. G
5. A
6. G
7. D
8. H
9. C
10. F
11. A
12. H
13. C
14. H
15. D
16. I
17. B
18. I
19. C
20. H

Unit 5 Matter and Its Changes

Lesson 1 Quiz, p. AG 46

1. A
2. I
3. B
4. F
5. B

Lesson 2 Quiz, p. AG 47

1. A
2. F
3. B
4. F
5. B

Unit 5 Benchmark Test, pp. AG 48–51

1. A
2. G
3. C
4. G
5. C
6. F
7. D
8. F
9. B
10. F
11. B
12. G
13. C
14. I
15. D
16. H
17. D
18. H
19. D
20. I

Unit 6 Energy and Its Uses

Lesson 1 Quiz, p. AG 54
1. B
2. I
3. A
4. F
5. C

Lesson 2 Quiz, p. AG 55
1. C
2. H
3. D
4. H
5. D

Lesson 3 Quiz, p. AG 56
1. C
2. H
3. B
4. G
5. D

Lesson 4 Quiz, p. AG 57
1. B
2. I
3. B
4. G
5. C

Unit 6 Benchmark Test, pp. AG 58–61
1. C
2. F
3. A
4. H
5. C
6. G
7. D
8. I
9. C
10. F
11. D
12. G
13. C
14. I
15. C
16. I
17. A
18. H
19. B
20. H

Unit 7 Heat

Lesson 1 Quiz, p. AG 64
1. B
2. I
3. A
4. H
5. C

Lesson 2 Quiz, p. AG 65
1. D
2. F
3. A
4. G
5. D

Lesson 3 Quiz, p. AG 66
1. D
2. F
3. B
4. G
5. C

Lesson 4 Quiz, p. AG 67
1. D
2. F
3. A
4. F
5. C

Unit 7 Benchmark Test, pp. AG 68–71
1. A
2. I
3. B
4. F
5. A
6. F
7. B
8. F
9. B
10. I
11. C
12. I
13. A
14. I
15. D
16. F
17. C
18. F
19. D
20. F

Unit 8 Forces and Motion

Lesson 1 Quiz, p. AG 74
1. B
2. G
3. D
4. G
5. B

Lesson 2 Quiz, p. AG 75
1. B
2. I
3. C
4. I
5. C

Unit 8 Benchmark Test, pp. AG 76–79
1. D
2. H
3. B
4. G
5. B
6. H
7. C
8. F
9. A
10. F
11. B
12. H
13. B
14. I
15. B
16. G
17. D
18. F
19. B
20. G

Unit 9 Life Cycles and Growth

Lesson 1 Quiz, p. AG 82
1. C
2. I
3. B
4. H
5. A

Lesson 2 Quiz, p. AG 83
1. D
2. H
3. A
4. F
5. D

Lesson 3 Quiz, p. AG 84
1. C   4. H
2. H   5. B
3. B

Lesson 4 Quiz, p. AG 85
1. D   4. H
2. H   5. C
3. C

Unit 9 Benchmark Test, pp. AG 86–89
1. A   8. F   15. D
2. H   9. D   16. H
3. C   10. H   17. C
4. G   11. C   18. G
5. D   12. H   19. C
6. H   13. B   20. G
7. C   14. I

Unit 10 Organisms and the Environment

Lesson 1 Quiz, p. AG 92
1. A   4. G
2. F   5. A
3. C

Lesson 2 Quiz, p. AG 93
1. B   4. F
2. F   5. B
3. B

Lesson 3 Quiz, p. AG 94
1. A   4. F
2. F   5. B
3. C

Lesson 4 Quiz, p. AG 95
1. D   4. I
2. F   5. B
3. C

Lesson 5 Quiz, p. AG 96
1. C   4. I
2. G   5. D
3. A

Unit 10 Benchmark Test, pp. AG 97–100
1. B   8. H   15. C
2. G   9. A   16. H
3. D   10. G   17. C
4. I   11. C   18. I
5. C   12. G   19. B
6. I   13. C   20. G
7. D   14. G

Florida Benchmark Practice Test A, pp. AG 103–115
1. C   11. C   21. B
2. I   12. F   22. F
3. D   13. C   23. C
4. G   14. F   24. G
5. A   15. B   25. B
6. G   16. F   26. H
7. B   17. C   27. C
8. I   18. I   28. I
9. B   19. D   29. B
10. H   20. I   30. I

Florida Benchmark Practice Test B, pp. AG 117–129
1. D   11. B   21. D
2. F   12. H   22. I
3. B   13. B   23. A
4. G   14. G   24. F
5. C   15. A   25. C
6. G   16. G   26. H
7. D   17. D   27. B
8. I   18. H   28. G
9. C   19. D   29. A
10. G   20. F   30. I

Florida Benchmark Practice Test C, pp. AG 131–143
1. C   11. D   21. A
2. I   12. I   22. H
3. D   13. B   23. B
4. H   14. F   24. G
5. A   15. D   25. C
6. G   16. H   26. G
7. D   17. A   27. B
8. I   18. H   28. I
9. A   19. D   29. D
10. I   20. I   30. H